WHAT OTHERS ARE SAYING...

"Julie has written a wonderful book for parents. She has covered several topics that are not commonly discussed that are very important to the health of children. Her common sense suggestions are refreshing. Thank you for your work, Julie!

- **Dr. Sherri Tenpenny, author, Saying No to Vaccines, and FOWL! Bird Flu: It's Not What You Think. President OsteoMed II www.osteomed2.com, and www.DrTenpenny.com**

"Parents of preschoolers need to make crucial decisions, some of which will have lifelong effects. Julie Cook prepares parents to make decisions about vaccination, school choices and television exposure using her own experience in a heartfelt, personal, and carefully reasoned process. The end result is some great parenting advice that makes perfect sense."

- **Randall Neustadter, OMD, author, Child Health Guide: Holistic Pediatrics for Parents, and The Vaccine Guide**

"I applaud you new book for its simplicity and ease of access. You invite the reader to step into the questions you asked, encourage them to ask the same and similar questions. The primary reason we don't is that we have been so deeply conditioned by the culture not to ask such questions. To ask them risks the wrath of the entire culture at every turn.

Indeed, yes it does take courage – that is, as long as you think the King has Clothes. There comes a moment when we pull back the curtain and see that the great and powerful OZ is just another snake oil salesman from Kansas... This insight changes everything."

- Michael Mendizza, author, Magical Parent-Magical Child: The Art of Joyful Parenting (co-authored with Joseph Chilton Pearce)

"If you want to make informed and from-the-heart parenting decisions without simply following the crowd, you're going to need this book."

- Diane Kidman, blogger, http://the-mommy-spot.blogspot.com/

"Julie Cook has written a valuable book to help parents make decisions that will affect their children for the rest of their lives. When Julie was pregnant with her first child, she found herself confronted with many decisions that, at first blush, seemed to be easy enough to make. Julie went to traditional schools herself and went on to college to obtain a couple masters degrees. She was also vaccinated as a child and had been exposed to plenty of television herself. But what Julie discovered is that her maternal intuition was peaking while she was pregnant, leading her to ask important questions and do her due diligence when researching for the answers.

The book starts out with Cord Blood Banking followed by a section on vaccines, then television and finally homeschooling. While Julie shares with her readers her journey of discovery that lead her to adopt unconventional ideas in raising her daughter, she is quick to mention that each parent must follow their own heart, intuition and gut instincts which may be different from hers.

The book is a page turner, carefully avoiding too much college-level scientific information so that parents will get the gist of her research quickly while being encouraged to follow through with research of their own. At the end of the book is an excellent reference section of pertinent books and articles to help parents get started.

The concept that I personally found most valuable was the idea of intrinsic versus extrinsic motivation in people. It is clear that through television and both private and public schools, we have created a society of primarily extrinsically motivated people. If our society is going to move in a positive, solution-oriented direction from what we have now, it will be due to the creativity of intrinsically motivated people - those who have the ability to think outside the box.

It was clear to me that the most difficult decision for the author to communicate was the decision to leave her daughter free from vaccines. While keeping each section short and to the point, she also wanted to effectively dispel the myth that vaccines are safe, effective and necessary. Since there is so much information on this particular topic, Julie put a lot of thought into getting parents the tools to think critically rather than simply give them a Vaccination 101 course in a few pages. She ends the vaccine section with the idea that she did not make a decision to not vaccinate but rather a decision to keep her daughter's immune system intact and her body uncontaminated with toxic chemicals, a positive decision.

At the close of Unvaccinated, Homeschooled and TV-Free, the author really delves into the psychology of making important parenting decisions and then dealing with parents who have found it easier to just go with the flow by doing what 95 percent of other parents are doing. I found this section to be the most valuable to me since she explains clearly why people will go along with what the majority of people are doing when the stakes are the highest, such as the decision to vaccinate a child even when faced with evidence of neurological damage and autoimmune disease as a probable outcome.

Vaccination Liberation board members and chapter leaders have often communicated their frustration to me regarding their inability to reach friends and family members with factual evidence on the harm caused by vaccines and wonder what they can do to be more effective. This section helped me to see just why our efforts will only reach those who have a passion for research and aren't afraid to make logical decisions that put them at odds with the majority.

This book is highly recommended to give to all pregnant moms, especially those having their first child. Encouraging women to follow their gut instincts and intuition is so important for the health, vitality and mental well being of their children. And if their intuition leads them to make unconventional decisions, they will find much corroborating evidence and support through Julie Cook's new book, Unvaccinated, Homeschooled and TV-Free."

- Ingri Cassel, director, Vaccination Liberation

Unvaccinated, Homeschooled, and TV-Free

It's Not Just for Fanatics and Zealots

Julie Cook

No Regrets Publishing
www.noregretspublishing.com

All inquiries should be sent to:
No Regrets Publishing
www.noregretspublishing.com
juliecook@noregretslifecoaching.com

ISBN 978-0-9843050-0-1
Printed in the United States of America
First Paperback Edition: January, 2010
Cover design by Michelle Dorris

Editing by Simon Presland
Simon Presland is a professional writer with almost 200 articles published in a variety of genres including travel, informational, inspirational, Christian, home repair, personality profile, interview, and teaching. For more information contact Simon at www.simonpresland.com or www.thewritechoice.org.

For Genevieve

Contents

He who joyfully marches in rank and file has already earned my contempt. He has been given a large brain by mistake, since for him the spinal cord would suffice. Albert Einstein

Introduction

As family-focused couples, we are in one of two stages in life. Either we're planning a family, or raising our children (no matter hold old they are). For most parents, this means reading books and magazines, seeking advice from our moms, dads, and siblings, talking to friends, and finding out what society has to say about the best way to raise our kids.

Seeking advice from immediate family is one thing, but do we really want complete strangers and so-called "experts" telling us what is in the best interest of our children? Whose "best interest" do these so-called "experts" have in mind?

Before my daughter, Genevieve, was born, I lived an average, risk-free life. I did what most people do; I accepted the consensus "expert" decisions and followed conventional opinions. Raising Genevieve, however, changed my outlook on life.

The book you are about to read explains why I decided to go against established opinions and practices. It will show you how I developed a unique decision making process as it relates to raising a child. It's about performing due diligence rather than blindly buying into mainstream opinions. After five years of research, contemplation, and listening to my intuition, I've learned to trust my own knowledge, experience, instinct, and feelings, even if they contradict what everyone else is doing.

In each chapter you will read about the unconventional decisions my husband and I have made in the raising of our daughter, who is five-years-old at the time of publishing. When you look at the topics in this book, they appear to be unrelated. But in reality they are closely related. The decisions we've made about each topic play a part in ensuring our daughter has the best possible chance of becoming a whole, healthy and balanced person who joyfully lives life to the fullest. I purposely kept each topic short so that busy people could read the book quickly. (I am currently working on expanding each topic into its own book for people who desire more detail.)

I am a researcher at heart. Most decisions I make in my life are the result of casting a wide net to collect reams of data, analyzing the data, and then selecting the most prudent option. My love for knowledge and learning has led me to acquire a Bachelor's degree, two Master's degrees, and a PhD.

Before I became pregnant with Genevieve, I had strong opinions about many topics involved in child rearing – all based on what the "professionals" predicated. Having spent many years in educational institutions, I thought children should spend more time in school – possibly year round – and the more homework the better. I thought that vaccines were an absolute *must*. I thought that buying Baby Einstein videos for six-month-old babies was a great way to give them a head start in life. I thought that banking cord blood was a no-brainer and should be done without hesitation. Before having my child, I wasn't forced to think hard about such topics; I didn't have the intuition and instincts that caused me to question mainstream information presented by the media.

When Genevieve was born, the magnitude of parenthood and its responsibility hit me like a slap in the face, and my look-beneath-the-covers personality suddenly came to life. If mainstream media was reporting that everybody was doing X, I was not likely to believe it without doing my own research. It was easy to become complacent and lazy about my own life, but I wasn't going to be that way with my daughter's.

I began to have strong feelings about topics that weren't based on anything rational. Some of them went against every opinion I had about raising Genevieve. These feelings, made up of intuition and instinct, propelled me to spend endless hours researching topics that didn't seem to need any research; they were topics that seemed to be set in stone with only *one* right approach.

I will share with you the alternate and controversial decisions – meaning they went against "professional opinions" – that my husband and I made for our daughter in four major areas. They are introduced in the order that we encountered them.

The first is cord blood banking. "To bank or not to bank?" was a decision we needed to make prior to the birth. Cord blood, is of great value to the baby when transferred from the umbilical cord to the newborn at the end of the birthing process. Umbilical cord blood contains a spectacular array of cells such as stem cells and cancer fighting T-cells. In the U.S., however, doctors clamp the umbilical cord before the blood can drain to the baby, depriving the newborn of these much needed cells. To make matters worse, cord blood banking companies come along and attempt to charge you a large amount to drain the cord blood and store it in a bank for you. Why do they charge so much for it? Because it contains a magnificent array of cells that have the potential to cure life threatening diseases. If the blood is so valuable that companies were formed to drain it and bank it and charge thousands of dollars to do so, wouldn't that blood be important for your baby at birth? Why pay to bank it when it actually belongs to your baby and can be given to your newborn freely in the delivery room?

The second major decision we encountered revolved around vaccinations, and I knew this would take a lot of time to research. U.S. companies are primarily profit driven, and investigating vaccination would require pouring over international studies from countries with socialized medicine. Why? Because, generally speaking, U.S.-based medical studies are conducted only if the results will prove profitable.

Let me give you an example. Let's say that a group of people believe that eating dandelions will cure obesity. As the idea spreads, more people try the "dandelion diet" and it works well for them. You might think that a U.S. company would conduct an actual study to determine if there really are benefits, but you would probably be wrong. If the results proved true, who would make money from this discovery? Nobody. Dandelions grow freely everywhere. They are a nuisance for homeowners and most people would pay to have someone come over and eat them. If a company conducted this study and they proved that eating dandelions did, in fact, cure obesity, they would have spent thousands or millions of dollars on a study that would never yield them a single dime. We would no longer have a need for diet drugs, or liposuction, or diet counselors – not to mention all of the medications prescribed for the side effects of being obese. Companies that produce these products and services would lose money and their stockholders would lose money. Since most companies are in business to make a profit, they wouldn't think

"Hmmmm...wouldn't it be great if dandelions *really* cured obesity? If that happened we wouldn't have to bother employing people to make obesity drugs, nor would we be concerned about increasing our profits. Life would be great for everyone!"

I have no issues with our profit driven society; it is an integral part of democracy. However, researching vaccines requires looking to countries with socialized medicine because, in most cases, they conduct research for the sake of getting answers, and not necessarily for profit.

After I had these important medical decisions thoroughly researched and out of the way, I began to look at a third major area – lifestyle decisions. At my baby shower, I received many Brainy Baby and Baby Einstein videos. People assumed that I'd want to give my daughter the much heralded "edge" over other children. I was happy to receive these gifts and had every intention of using them as soon as Genevieve's eyes could focus. But, something didn't feel quite right. My brain believed it was a perfect idea but some intangible part of me was holding out. This started me down a path of researching the effects of videos, television, and all screen-based media on infants and children.

In this section, I describe the results of various studies revolving around the media itself as well as the impact of commercials and marketing on children. But you will see that, ultimately, my decision was not based on any studies or research. Instead of deciding what I *did not* want for my daughter, I focused on what I *did* want for her – how I wanted her to spend her time and how I wanted her to interact with her environment. No matter what the studies reported, I had to ask myself, "Is it better to actively engage in life or spend time watching others do so?"

The forth major area and lifestyle decision my husband and I made concerned the type of education Genevieve would receive. I outline the top ten reasons why I decided to homeschool her. Of these reasons, not one of them has to do with what is being taught at school, religious beliefs (I'm not overtly religious), political views, or the increasingly violent atmosphere of schools. As with all decisions we made concerning our daughter, we decided to do what we thought was best for her, even if we went against societies "norms."

As you read this book, my hope is that you will glean insight from our decision-making process that will help you make the best decisions for your own family, rather than following mainstream mindsets. In following my own path of parenthood, I've noticed that, when I tell people of my decisions, they immediately defend the paths they have chosen. I do not want to put anyone on the defensive. But I would like to give you some food for thought and help you think outside of the box. If I wear a green shirt and you wear blue, we don't need to justify our decision, nor pass judgment. We may ask each other about our choice of color, and we may agree or disagree. But, in the end, we must decide what is best for us. I'm not anti-vaccine, anti-school, or anti-TV.....I'm anti-complacency.

Please keep an open mind as you read through the chapters. If you've come to conclusions or make decisions that are opposite to mine, try to be cognizant of your mind's ability to justify or rationalize your actions. Try to discover your reasoning. If you feel the need to defend your position, it is possible that you are not truly at peace with your decisions, meaning your brain is not in alignment with your heart and soul. Hopefully, my book will bring you to a place of peace with your parenting decisions.

Let your previously established mindsets be challenged as you read each chapter. By the time you finish the book, you'll have greater understanding and firmer convictions about the way you are raising your children (or plan to raise your children). But be prepared; you may also find yourself changing some of your conventional and cherished ideas, or at the very least, embarking on a long journey of research for yourself.

Happy reading!

Intuition becomes increasingly valuable in the new information society precisely because there is so much data. John Naisbitt

Cord Blood Banking

In 2004, when I was pregnant with Genevieve, umbilical cord blood banking was in vogue. Parents with the money to bank the blood were eagerly doing so. The media was reporting on the miracle of stem cells and banking a newborn's blood was a way to preserve those precious stem cells for the future. They have the potential to fight and/or treat serious diseases, and what better gift could a parent give to a child? Most media reporting led the general public to believe that the new phenomena definitely should be done, assuming you had the money.

When I became pregnant, I had the money to follow this trend, and I intended to do so. Why not store the blood in case my daughter needed it in the future? It seemed like common sense. Everything I heard on the news and read in magazines touted the importance of storing this valuable resource. I made the decision without hesitation. Why wouldn't I?

But when I started researching cord blood banking companies and talking to their representatives, something didn't *feel* right. I had no reason to think it wasn't the right thing to do; I had never heard anyone question the idea, and there were no "cons" brought up in the media, other than the cost. Still…..something *inside me* wasn't convinced.

I was very busy with work, and school (I was working on my PhD and my job was requiring 60+ hours per week) and I really didn't have time to start questioning my decision. Questioning the decision would mean I'd have to thoroughly research the topic which would take days and weeks. While, I loved to research and arrive at answers, it was very time consuming. So, when the odd twinges of doubt began to haunt my mind, I took the easy way out and ignored them. It was *easier* for me to ignore them. That way, I could go about my life, with work and school and thinking of baby names. *Besides*, I thought, *I don't want to immerse myself in research that would likely lead to more questions than answers, requiring even more research.* I didn't have time for all of that! I didn't *want* to make time for all of that! It was *easier* to believe what was reported in mainstream media. Plus, if I made a decision based on accepted opinion, I couldn't possibly be blamed if it turned out to be wrong. *Everyone else* was doing it, or so it seemed.

Why, then, were all the conversations I had with the cord blood banking companies so unsettling? Whenever I compared the prices of each bank and looked into the features they offered, those nagging doubts would butt against my logical thinking. Initially, I thought I was having issues with the cost, much like buyer's remorse. But I hadn't bought anything.

What was *really* bothering me? I had enough money to afford to bank my daughter's blood, and had spent more money on crazier things, or so I thought. Nonetheless, I knew something about the cost was bothering me. On the surface, it seemed like the smart thing to do. But after mulling my decision over for a couple of weeks, I had an epiphany. Why would I pay money to bank something that *already belongs* to my child? That broke the "question dam" wide open. Wouldn't my child get all of that precious blood anyway since it's in her umbilical cord? Why is it taken from her at birth? If the blood is so valuable that people will pay to store it, then isn't it invaluable to her when she's first born? Shouldn't she receive it immediately rather than saving it for later?

No matter how late it was at night, or how many hours I'd worked that day, thinking through these questions energized me. I knew I was on the right track. My inner being was responding favorably to this line of questioning and my feelings were fueling me, driving me toward answers. I began my research based on all of these questions. What follows is not intended to be an all-inclusive, definitive findings report. Rather, it is a very small sample of the type of information I found in libraries, medical journals, and more. I encourage everyone to do their own research and draw your own conclusions.

When a baby is born, doctors in the U.S. tie or clamp the umbilical cord almost immediately. This ensures that most, if not all, of the cord blood *never* makes it to the baby. This is the blood that is banked; the cord is clamped and the blood is taken from the umbilical cord and banked, if you have purchased cord blood banking. If the cord blood is not banked, it is thrown away! I first heard this while talking to one of the largest cord banking companies. I asked the woman on the phone whether or not the baby needs the cord blood at birth, or if it's okay for it to be taken from her. The lady replied "it must be okay to take it at birth because if the blood isn't banked, then the doctors just throw it away anyway." Huh? They throw it away? Yep. The umbilical cord is clamped right away when the baby is born and the trapped blood is thrown out.

Early cord clamping is a "recent" medical trend, which has only been practiced since the 1940s and only in a few countries, including the U.S. Early cord clamping is not natural, normal, or based on any evolutionary need. In 1801 Erasmus Darwin (one of the most important physician's and intellectuals of his time) was one of the first to urge that cord clamping not occur until all cord pulsation ceased. Clamping the cord early is an interruption of a natural process. There is *no* evidence to show it is beneficial to the baby in any way. The World Health Organization states, "Late clamping (or not clamping at all) is the physiological way of treating the cord, and early clamping is an intervention that needs justification." [1]

Umbilical cord blood is a baby's life blood until birth. This blood contains magnificent cells such as red blood cells, stem cells and cancer-fighting T-cells. It comes from the placenta since the umbilical cord is attached to it. The placenta really belongs to the baby; it is one of the baby's organs while the baby is growing inside the mother. When a baby is born and the umbilical cord is cut quickly, it is akin to amputating a live organ from a person. It is the same as submitting the newborn to severe hemorrhaging. If the umbilical cord is not cut, the placenta will expire naturally in an hour or so, after the blood has fully drained into the baby. [2]

When the umbilical cord is cut early, the valuable cord blood, rich in stem cells and red blood cells, never makes it to the newborn. The deprivation of placental blood results in a relatively large loss of iron to the infant. If cord clamping is

---

[1] World Health Organization (1996). Care in Normal Birth: A Practical Guide.
[2] De Marsh, Q.B, (1941). The Effect of Depriving the Infant of its Placental Blood. *Journal of American Medical Association*, 116(23), 2568-2573.

eliminated or delayed, allowing the blood to flow into the infant, the baby receives increased levels of iron and has a lower risk of anemia.[3] Also, there are fewer transfusions needed and fewer incidences of intraventricular hemorrhage. Even if cord clamping is delayed by two-minutes, the baby's iron reserve is doubled, which is equivalent to two months of an infant's iron requirements. This helps prevent iron deficiency from developing prior to six months of age. [4]

Not clamping the umbilical cord is beneficial to *all* babies. However, it's most beneficial for infants with low birth weights, infants born to iron-deficient mothers, or premature babies. Mother-nature provides babies with breast milk for good reasons, and she provides iron-rich placental blood for good reasons as well.[5] You may have noticed that baby formula companies promote their products as ways to guard against iron deficiency. Now, why would a baby have an iron deficiency? Oh yes...because the cord was clamped early, cutting off the baby's iron supply.

Please keep in mind that this information is just a small sample of the published data showing that umbilical cord blood is valuable to the baby and harm is done when the baby does not receive it (see the References section at the end of this book for information on source data). The benefits of the cells in cord

---

[3] Piscane, A. (1996). Neonatal prevention of iron deficiency. *BMJ*, *312*, 136-137.

[4] Gupta, R., Ramji, S. (2001). Effect of delayed cord clamping on iron stores in infants born to anemic mothers: A randomized controlled trial. *Indian Pediatrics, 39,* 130-135.

[5] Hutton, E., PhD, Hassan, E. S. (2007). Late vs. early clamping of the umbilical cord in full-term neonates: Systematic review and meta-analysis of controlled trials. *The Journal of the American Medical Association. 297*, 1241-1252.

blood are not fully known as of yet, making it even *more* important for the baby to receive its own cord blood.

After finishing my research, everything became crystal clear. My daughter *needs* that blood at *birth*. Let's look at the facts:

- There is no benefit to clamping the cord early (other than getting the patient out of the hospital room so that it can be used for the next patient, or freeing up the doctor so he/she can move on to the next patient).

- Clamping the cord is harmful to the baby because she doesn't get the valuable red cells, stem cells, iron, etc.

- Early clamping is what allows cord blood banking companies to take *my* baby's blood and then turn around and charge me to store it in case *my* baby needs it.

So, to bank or not-to-bank? To make this decision, I had to look at not only what was known, but also what was still unknown. On the *unknown* side I listed the following:

1. Would my baby suffer illnesses and disorders in her life due to *not* receiving her own cord blood at birth?

2. If I banked the cord blood, would my child ever need it in the future? Would it even help her?

3. Would denying my infant her cord blood at birth help create the very disorders that could later be cured by banking the blood?

On the *known* side I wrote:

1. Letting my baby have her own cord blood at birth would not cause *any* harm at all.

2. Giving my baby her own cord blood at birth would enhance her health.

Profitability Path

I also went down the profitability path and asked myself these questions:

1. If I don't bank the cord blood, does anyone profit? No, they do not.

2. If I choose to bank the blood, who profits? The cord blood banking companies, their employees, and people who hold the stock in these companies.

3. If I ask that the umbilical cord be clamped only after all blood drains into the baby, does anyone stand to *lose* money from that decision? Yes. The hospitals would lose money. New mothers would need to remain in their rooms longer, along with their doctors, so new patients could not be moved in. Allowing my daughter to keep her own blood meant people and companies would lose money. If you think about this from a longer term perspective, even more people stand to lose money. Since giving infants their cord blood may mean fewer diseases and fewer medical treatments needed in the future, you can be assured that an astonishing amount of money will be lost by the companies that make their survival off of sick people.

Whenever money is at stake, there is the potential for deception, abuse or hidden agendas. I'm not saying any of this is happening; I'm only pointing out that the potential exists, and this can play into the decision making process.

At the end of my research, I'd reached some definite conclusions. I knew that my baby needed her cord blood and denying it would be harmful to her. I also knew that giving my baby her own cord blood would deny profits and cause monetary losses for others. There is no incentive for anyone to come right out and tell me that my baby needs her cord blood, and not to allow early cord clamping. If I was going to make the decision to let my baby keep her valuable blood, I should not expect anything in the mainstream media to echo that decision.

I finally decided to allow my daughter to keep what is rightfully hers—her own, naturally enriched blood. When I made that decision, I had no more odd feelings, twinges of doubt or unidentifiable anxiety. Everything felt perfectly in alignment.

After I made the decision, I double-checked my thinking and wrote down what would have to be true in order for me to *want* to bank my baby's cord blood.

1. I would need to be positive that denying the cord blood at birth would cause her *no* harm.

2. I would have to be fairly certain that banking the blood would be useful to her, or a sibling, at some point in the future.

Since neither of those is even partially true, I was convinced that my decision was sound.

Before my daughter was born, I told my doctor that the cord is not to be cut until all cord blood had drained into the baby and the cord stops pulsating. The doctor understood and agreed. During the birth, my husband was prepared to intervene should he notice that the cord was still pulsating when the doctor attempted to clamp it.

It was important that I had listened to my inner voice. Had I banked the blood, everything may have turned out fine. However, the harmony that I felt when I finally got my decision into alignment with my instincts was very gratifying and brought with it an indescribable peace. In this particular instance, my inner voice came to me in a way that was really nothing more than a feeling. It would have been very easy to ignore and I'm certain I've ignored many similar feelings in the past. However, once I listened to it, my inner voice began to call out to me louder and louder as time went on. I found that the more in tune I became with it, the more it voiced its opinions and ideas.

The cord blood banking decision was a very easy one. Now, let's move on to a much more difficult decision – to vaccinate…or not?

Your time is limited, so don't waste it living someone else's life. Don't be trapped by dogma which is living with the results of other people's thinking. Don't let the noise of other's opinions drown out your own inner voice. Steve Jobs

Vaccines

As the birth of Genevieve grew close, I began looking for a pediatrician. I knew that shortly after she was born, I would "have to" schedule the routine appointments for her immunizations. Thinking about immunizations made me mildly anxious. I spoke to friends in the area who had young children to see who they were using. Within the course of those conversations, friends would say things like "Whoever you go to, be prepared because it's very traumatic to see your child go through that" or "I go to so-and-so because my child always has a bad reaction to vaccines. My Dr. lives close to me and I can get my child to the office right away."

Now, those types of comments may seem completely normal to everyone. When I asked questions of my friends, they said things like "Yes, it's hard to see your child confused about why you are subjecting her to pain and crying but she has to go through it and she'll forget about it right away."

She has to go through it? Why?, I thought. Then, a friend said "Even though it's painful and there could be bad reactions, vaccines save many lives in the long run." *Really? Save many lives? Says who? How do you know that? Did the doctor present conclusive studies and facts that convinced you? Did he even present semi-conclusive studies?*

I was 38 at the time and my days were completely filled with work, school and pregnancy. I was always tired and frequently looked for the "easy way out." Because of that, I looked for every opportunity to go with the flow, because everything else took too much time and energy. Sometimes I found myself *purposefully* not thinking about troubling topics and busying myself as an avoidance tactic. For far too long, I just assumed I would vaccinate my baby and whenever questions crept up, I'd dive into work or school.

Throughout my pregnancy, every doctor I saw just *assumed* I would be vaccinating my child. However, no doctor ever attempted to tell me about the benefits of vaccines, or show me any confirmed evidence of benefits, nor did they go through major studies proving and/or disproving the benefits. It's taken for granted that *everyone knows* the benefits and *everyone believes* the pro-vaccine propaganda. In fact, had I asked any one of my doctors to cite a major study definitively proving that vaccines saved lives, not one of them could have done so.

At this point, I didn't know much, but I listed what I did know:

1. Vaccines are painful for babies and young children

2. Some children experience negative reactions to vaccines

3. Doctors and the media talk about vaccines as if there is no alternative to vaccinating. There is a heavy push toward vaccinating throughout the media and medical industries.

4. There's a lot of money to be made producing and administering vaccines.

I also listed what I didn't know:

1. Do vaccines save lives and what proof is there?

2. Are vaccines safe? Are any of the ingredients harmful in the short or long-term?

3. How does the health of vaccinated people compare to the health of non-vaccinated people?

4. Why does the media and medical industry push so heavily for vaccines? Is the life-saving evidence and volume of conclusive studies so plentiful as to make vaccinating "a given" for anyone with half a brain?

Oh great! Now there was no going back. The unknowns were deep and the knowns were few. Why, oh why, couldn't I just go along with what everyone else was doing and just trust the media and the medical industry to tell me what's best for my daughter? It would be so easy and convenient. And, if I went along with what everyone else was doing and I was wrong…it wouldn't be my fault, would it? After all, everyone else was doing it so wouldn't it be *their* fault for misleading me and pushing me down this path? Sure it would. I can just go about my normal life and wrap this decision up right now.

But…what if my daughter got gravely ill from a vaccine or developed some disease later in life that was linked to a vaccine, or died young with a possible vaccine link? Would I feel guilt-free, knowing that everyone else basically made the vaccination decision for me? Would I truly be able to say "Well, nobody saw that coming; I couldn't have possibly known; I didn't really have a *choice* at the time." Here's the problem with "going with the flow"; if you haven't begun to think for yourself and don't yet let your inner voice guide you toward questions and answers, and if you are used to living through the opinions and "facts" spewed by others, then you can continue to live in ignorant bliss. But, if you've passed way beyond that point and are familiar with the whole breadth of your life choices, and you understand that only you are fully accountable and responsible for your decisions, then you can't turn back. Your decisions are made using all of the available tools, including instinct, intuition, feelings, knowledge, and data.

Once again, I began investigating a topic that everyone else seemed to already know the answer to - which was, of course, to vaccinate. And, what I found was shocking.

First, let me say that there is a lifetime worth of content to sort through when it comes to vaccines. I will summarize a small portion of what I found, but please know that this is just the tiniest sample of what is available (see the References section at the end of this book for information on source data). Anyone thinking about the potentially life altering decision to vaccinate their child should absolutely listen to their own inner voice and do the type of research that will answer their own questions and get them to a place where the information in their head matches their feelings and intuition and heart.

Diseases Declined Before Vaccines

The diseases that we vaccinate against were declining well before vaccines were even introduced. In fact, there was a drop-off well over 200 years ago which was long before vaccines were introduced. The decline is attributed to improved nutrition and hygiene of the population in general. The statistics reported by pharmaceutical companies that seem to show diseases declined once a vaccine was introduced are not entirely accurate; the statistics start at a time when the diseases were already declining rapidly. For example, if a disease was declining on its own for fifteen years and then a vaccine was introduced, the pharmaceutical company starts quoting statistics based on the date the vaccine was introduced – fifteen years after the decline of the disease, in this example. This makes it look like the vaccine had something to do with the decline. In fact, conclusive studies reveal that each introduction of a new vaccine has obtained only one *proven* result and that result is the immediate recurrence of the disease that the vaccine was intended to prevent.[6]

Now, if you vaccinated your children, as most people have, you don't want to read this. If you didn't vaccinate your children or don't intend to vaccinate them, you may still not want to read this. Digesting this type of information is extremely difficult and requires a lot from a person. It requires opening your mind and allowing or accepting new ideas and possibilities. It involves feeling very uncomfortable for unidentifiable reasons; becoming anxious and defensive; being willing to entertain the notion that the health of your child is not of primary importance

---

[6] Mendelsohn, R., M.D. (1987). *How to raise a healthy child in spite of your doctor.* New York: Ballantine Books.

to "everyone" in the pharmaceutical industry, medical community, and government agencies; and it means being willing to consider the possibility that *you may have done something that could harm your child.* Regardless, making an effort to dig up pertinent information is required. Below is a very small sample of the information available.

- In 1975 the pertussis (whooping cough) vaccination was stopped in Germany. Therefore, fewer than 10 percent of children in Germany are vaccinated against pertussis. The number of cases of pertussis has steadily declined since 1975 even though far fewer children are receiving the pertussis vaccine.[7]

- In 1986 the state of Kansas had 1300 cases of pertussis and 90 percent of the cases occurred in children who were vaccinated. There has been universal vaccination against pertussis in Nova Scotia but pertussis continues to occur there. In the Netherlands, over 96 percent of the children have been receiving the pertussis vaccine for over twenty years and pertussis remains an endemic there. Children there receive three pertussis shots by the age of twelve months.[8]

---

[7] Baker, Jeffrey (2002). *The pertussis controversy in Great Britain, 1974-1986.* Center for the Study of Medical Ethics and Humanities. Duke University.

[8] De Melker, H.E., Schellekens, J.F., Neppelenbroek, S.E., Mooi, F.R., Rumke, H.C., Conyn-van Spaendonck, M.A. (2000). *Reemergence of pertussis in the highly vaccinated population of the Netherlands: observations on surveillance data.* Department of Infectious Disease Epidemiology, National Institute of Public Health and the Environment. Bilthoven, the Netherlands.

Vaccines

- In 1958, the United States had about 800,000 cases of the measles but by 1962, the number of cases dropped to 300,000. In 1963, the measles vaccine was introduced but the disease had already rapidly declined in the five years before the vaccine was made available. During the next four years, the measles continued declining at the same pace. In 1955, before the measles vaccine was introduced, the death rate from measles was .03 per 100,000 in the U.S. In 1990, there were 13.3 measles deaths per 100,000 in the U.S. In England, the measles mortality rate declined by 97 percent before the vaccination was instituted.[9]

- There have been measles outbreaks in U.S. schools where vaccination rates are over 98 percent. These outbreaks occurred in places where no previously reported cases of measles had been reported for several years. An outbreak of measles occurred in a school where 100 percent of the children had been vaccinated.[9]

- In 1911, the Metropolitan Life Insurance Company reported that the four leading causes of childhood deaths from infectious diseases in the U.S. were diphtheria, scarlet fever, pertussis and measles. By 1945, before the mass vaccine programs were introduced for those diseases, the combined death rates had already declined by 95 percent.[10]

---

[9] Tenpenny, Sherri, M.D. (2003). *Vaccines: What CDC Documents and Science Reveal*. RJ Media Magic.
[10] Creighton, C., M.D. (2009). *The vaccination myth: Courageous M.D. exposes the vaccination fraud*. CA: Createspace.

- In 1925, the diphtheria vaccine was introduced in Germany. After the introduction, the cases of diphtheria steadily increased until Germany halted them shortly after the Second World War. When the vaccine was halted, there was a decline in diphtheria. Once the disease had slowed way down, Germany reintroduced the vaccine.[11]

- The polio vaccine was introduced in England in 1956 but the incidence of polio had decreased by 82 percent in the years before the vaccine was made available.[12]

- In one year in England, 97.5 percent of people between the ages of two and fifty were vaccinated against smallpox. The following year, England experienced the worst smallpox epidemic in its history with 44,840 deaths. In a six-year period after the smallpox vaccine was introduced, the incidences of smallpox rose from 28 to 46 per 100,000 people.[13]

- Medical journals around the world have already documented proof that vitamin C has consistently cured both acute polio and acute hepatitis, which are two diseases that modern medicine still refers to as incurable.[14]

---

[11] Coleman, Vernon., M.D. The Vernon Colman Health Letter. www.vernoncoleman.com/vaccines.htm.

[12] Miller, Neil Z. (2002). *Vaccines: Are they really safe and effective?* Santa Fe, NM: New Atlantean Press.

[13] Ruata, Charles, M.D. (1904). A summary of the proofs that vaccination does not prevent smallpox but really increases it. National Anti-Vaccination League, S616.

[14] Tenpenny, Sherri, M.D. (2008). *Saying No to Vaccines.* NMA Media Press.

- Nearly every disease that is vaccinated against would not be deadly or serious if contracted today.

Remember that what I have written above is just the smallest fraction of research available. For each of the points listed, there are hundreds of pages of related research and studies that do exist and they are proven and credible. They just don't get publicized for reasons we will discuss soon.

In summary, nearly every disease was in decline *before* vaccination programs began. The reason for the decline may have been improved nutrition, better quality water, higher standards of living, and less crowded living conditions. Not only were the diseases seeing a decline, they were seeing *rapid* and *dramatic* declines that were in proportion to the speed with which nutrition and living conditions were improving. Not only were the diseases already declining before vaccinations were started, but the onset of some vaccine programs caused epidemics and extreme increases in the diseases the vaccines were created to prevent.

At this point, I can say that at best, we know that vaccines did not cause diseases to decline; they were declining well before vaccines were introduced. At worst, vaccines don't work and they can cause an increase in the diseases they were meant to prevent.

Vaccine Risks

If someone asked me to inject myself with formaldehyde, would I do it? I don't think so. If the person then told me that it *might* protect me against a disease I'm *unlikely* to get, and that the disease is rare and unlikely to be harmful or serious,…would that sweeten the pot for me and make me want to inject something like formaldehyde into myself?

Have you ever asked a doctor what level of formaldehyde or mercury is safe to inject or ingest? There are many toxic ingredients in vaccines that doctors would tell you are unsafe at any level. Some of the main ones are formaldehyde, mercury, aspartame (which converts into formaldehyde once inside your body), polysorbate-80, silicon, thimerosal, aluminum.

What's that you say? You heard the vaccine makers stopped putting mercury in vaccines? Not so. In 1999 many vaccine makers volunteered to start producing "mercury free" vaccines. Some claimed their vaccines only contained trace amounts. However, when testing was done by the Health Advocacy in the Public Interest (HAPI) of supposed "mercury free" vials, all of the vials contained mercury. They also contained thimerosal, a 50 percent mercury compound. In addition, they all contained aluminum. Aluminum vastly enhances the toxicity of mercury, which causes neuronal death in the brain.

The mercury content in vaccines has been linked to the autism epidemic as well as other neurological disorders impacting children. A causal relationship has not been proven and is unlikely to ever be proven given the myriad of toxic ingredients in vaccines. What is interesting is that one in every 150 children in the United States has a life-long autism spectrum disorder *except* among the Amish. The Amish don't vaccinate.

Here's an interesting fact about mercury. In the 19th century, hat makers used mercury in the making of hats. The mercury adversely affected the nervous systems of the hat makers which caused trembling muscles, twitching limbs, distorted vision, aggressiveness, hallucinations and other psychotic behaviors. Hat makers became known as "mad hatters" because the mercury exposure caused them to appear insane.

The FDA does not consider mercury to be a safe enough substance to include as a food additive or in over-the-counter drug products. But, the FDA deems mercury safe enough to include in vaccines that are given to babies without developed immune systems. Most infants receive as many as fifteen doses of mercury-containing vaccines before the age of six months. It is not possible that this level of mercury could reside in an infant's body without causing serious disruptions.

Some of the research findings are shown below. As I have always said, don't take my word for it and don't rely on my research; this is important enough that you should do your own digging. This section shows a fraction of what I found in medical journals around the world, and this information helped guide me toward my decision and got me to a point where what my brain knew, was in alignment with my inner voice.

- An unpublished Canadian study in 2009, looked at 12 million people and found that getting the seasonal flu vaccine, as recommended by the U.S. CDC and NIH, doubles one's risk of developing the H1N1 infection (Swine Flu) and makes the infection much more serious. [15]

---

[15] British Columbia Centre for Disease Control and Laval University (2009). Seasonal Flu Shot Linked to H1N1.

33

- According to the results of a large Australian study, the risk of developing encephalitis from the pertussis vaccine was five times greater than the risk of developing encephalitis by contacting pertussis by natural methods.[16]

- In New Zealand after an aggressive vaccine program against hepatitis B was implemented, the incidence of Type 1 diabetes in children rose by 61 percent. Similar studies done in England, Italy, Denmark and Sweden show similar results. The U.S. recently started the same vigorous vaccine program against hepatitis B.[17]

- In December 2000, U.S. children aged two months began receiving the hepatitis B vaccine and most newborns now receive the hepatitis B vaccine in the hospital. No study was ever done to determine if the vaccine was safe for children of this age. Approximately 10 percent of all adverse vaccine reactions are ever reported by doctors. Over 36,000 adverse reactions and 440 deaths were soon reported, which represents roughly 10 percent of the actual adverse reactions and deaths from the vaccine. The CDC's Chief of Epidemiology has said that serious reaction to hepatitis B vaccine is ten times higher than other vaccines. Hepatitis B is transmitted sexually and through contaminated blood so the incidence of two-month old children contracting hepatitis B must be very close to zero.[18]

---

[16] Creighton, C., M.D. (2009). The vaccination myth: Courageous M.D. exposes the vaccination fraud. CA: Createspace.
[17] Tenpenny, Sherri, M.D. (2008). *Saying No to Vaccines*. NMA Media Press.
[18] Miller, Neil Z. (2002). *Vaccines: Are they really safe and effective?* Santa Fe, NM: New Atlantean Press.

Vaccines

- On January 26, 1988, the Washington Post reported that *all* cases of polio since 1979 were caused by the polio vaccine; not one case of polio reported since 1979 was caused by a wild strain. [19]

- In 1955, it was concluded that sulpha drugs and vaccination are directly responsible for the production of leukemia in humans. No contradictory studies or evidence exist.[20]

- In Cracow, Poland, the smallpox vaccination has been shown to manifest as leukemia in both children and adults.[11]

- A study done in 1978 proved that adults who had natural measles had a decreased incidence of various diseases including Parkinson's Disease.[21]

- A study done in 1985 showed that when mumps are contracted in childhood, a woman has a far lesser chance of contracting ovarian cancer.[22]

- The incidence of Sudden Infant Death syndrome (SIDS) rose from .55 per 1000 live births in 1953 to 12.8 per

[19] Creighton, C., M.D. (2009). The vaccination myth: Courageous M.D. exposes the vaccination fraud. CA: Createspace.
[20] Mendelsohn, R., M.D. (1987). *How to raise a healthy child in spite of your doctor.* New York: Ballantine Books.
[21] Sasco AJ, Paffenbarger RS Jr. (1985). Measles infection and Parkinson's disease. *Am J Epidemiol. 1985 Dec;122(6):1017-31.*
[22] Tenpenny, Sherri, M.D. (2008). *Saying No to Vaccines.* NMA Media Press

1000 in 1992 in Olmstead County, Minnesota. 85 percent of SIDS cases occur in the first six months of life with the peak incidence being two to four months which is the exact time most vaccines are given. Total infant deaths from SIDS has risen from 2.5 per 1000 in 1953 to 17.9 per 1000 in 1992 which was the time period when vaccines per child rose steadily to 36.[23]

- The rise in the number of childhood vaccines has coincided with an identical rise in the incidence of auto-immune diseases seen in children such as rheumatoid arthritis, lupus, psoriasis, asthma, multiple sclerosis. [23]

- Naturally acquired immunity by acquiring an illness involves a virus spreading from the respiratory tract to the liver, thymus, spleen and bone marrow. At the first sign of symptoms, the entire immune system responds to repel the virus and during that process the immune system creates antibodies that provide life-long immunity against that virus. The child is then prepared to respond quickly to an infection by the same virus in the future. Vaccination does not do this. They create a situation that provokes auto-immune reactions in the body.[23]

- All reported cases of macrophagic myofasciitis - a disease that causes pain in muscles, bones, and joints - have been reported in people who received vaccines containing aluminum.[23]

---

[23] Howenstine, James, M.D. (2009). Why you should avoid taking vaccines. http://www.safe2use.com/ca-ipm/09-29-07.htm

- Aluminum has been shown to remain in the body and disrupt the immune and nervous system for a lifetime.[24]

- When pertussis (whooping cough vaccine) is injected into animals, it leads to insulin disorders. In 1979, a study was done that showed the same result in humans. Insulin disorders, such as juvenile diabetes, hypoglycemia, and adult diabetes have been rising since the pertussis vaccine was introduced.[25]

- The following conditions are on the rise *only* in countries with aggressive vaccine programs: autism spectrum disorders, leukemia, cancers, brain tumors, allergies, impulsive violence, diabetes, Crohn's disease, asthma, and information processing disorders. All of these conditions are rare in countries without aggressive vaccine programs.[26]

- In the early 1900s, one Indiana physician reported that he had seen more than 200 cases of cancer in his practice and all were among vaccinated people. He didn't have one case of cancer among his unvaccinated patients.[27]

---

[24] Volpe, Arturo, M.D. (2009). Natural health solutions. http://www.doctorvolpe.com/
[25] Coulter, Harris Ph.D. (1997). Childhood vaccinations and juvenile-onset (type 1) diabetes. http://www.whale.to/v/coulter.html
[26] Howenstine, James, M.D. (2009). Why you should avoid taking vaccines. http://www.safe2use.com/ca-ipm/09-29-07.htm
[27] Eisenstein, Mayer M.D. (2008). *Don't vaccinate before you educate.* CMI Press.

- One physician noted that his unvaccinated children were healthier and hardier than their vaccinated peers. Allergies, asthma, behavioral disorders, and attentional disturbances were non-existent among his unvaccinated patients and they were somewhat common among his vaccinated patients.[27]

- One physician noted that cancer was not present in any of his unvaccinated children or adults – not one. Only his vaccinated children and adults had any cancers. The explanation for this was already known and well documented in medical journals. All vaccines given over a short period of time to an immature immune system (mainly children's immune systems) deplete the thymus gland of irreplaceable immune cells. The primary gland involved in immune reactions is the thymus gland. In an immature immune system, every immune cell multiples to form a strong, mature immune system that will fight off the growth of abnormal cells (such as cancer cells). When the immune cells are depleted by vaccines, they cannot multiply the way needed to effectively fight off infection and abnormal cell growth.[27]

- The Arthur Research Foundation in Tucson, Arizona has shown that up to 60 percent of the immune system is exhausted by multiple vaccinations, leaving only 40 percent of the immune system in tact to fight off infection and abnormal cell growth. In unvaccinated children, only 10 percent of the immune cells are lost when a child is permitted to develop natural immunity from diseases, meaning they keep 90 percent of their immune cells in tact. Infectious diseases are much less likely to attack and kill those who have healthy immune systems. [28]

- A New Zealand study disclosed that 23 percent of vaccinated children develop asthma, as compared to 0 percent in unvaccinated children.[28]

- There is no scientific proof that any vaccine is safe. We only have epidemiologic studies which are not the same as scientific proof of safety.[29]

- A single vaccine given to a six-pound newborn is the *equivalent of giving a 180-pound adult 30 vaccinations on the same day*. Include in this the toxic effects of high levels of aluminum and formaldehyde contained in some vaccines, and the synergist toxicity could be increased to unknown levels. Further, it is very well known that infants do not produce significant levels of bile or have adult renal capacity for several months after birth. Bilary transport is the major biochemical route by which mercury is removed from the body, and infants cannot do this very well. They also do not possess the renal (kidney) capacity to remove aluminum. Additionally, mercury is a well-known inhibitor of kidney function.[30]

---

[28] Howenstine, James, M.D. (2009). Why you should avoid taking vaccines. http://www.safe2use.com/ca-ipm/09-29-07.htm
[29] Tenpenny, Sherri, M.D. (2008). *Saying No to Vaccines*. NMA Media Press
[30] Haley, Boyd (2001). *Committee for Government Reform presented on May 23, 2001 by Boyd Haley, Professor and Chair, Department of Chemistry, University of Kentucky*

- Dr. James R. Shannon, the former director of the National Institute of Health has said "the only safe vaccine is one that is never used."

- Dr. J. Anthony Morris, former Chief Vaccine Control Officer and research virologist for US FDA said "There is a great deal of evidence to prove that immunization of children does more harm than good."

- Dr. J. Anthony Morris, former Chief Vaccine Control Officer and research virologist for US FDA said "There is no evidence that any influenza vaccine thus far developed is effective in preventing or mitigating any attack of influenza. The producers of these vaccines know that they are worthless, but they go on selling them, anyway."

The best way to determine the risk/benefit profile of vaccination is to take a group of vaccinated children and compare them with an unvaccinated group of children with all other factors being equal. A study comparing vaccinated to unvaccinated children has never been done for *any* vaccine. Because these studies have never been done, vaccination is really just a massive experiment on our children.[31]

Again, this is a small amount of what is available. In the previous section, I discussed the fact that nearly every disease was declining before vaccination programs were introduced. In addition, nearly every disease vaccinated against would not be deadly or serious if contracted today. In this section, you can see there is much research around the fact that vaccines cause harm –

---

[31] Eisenstein, Mayer M.D. (2008). *Don't vaccinate before you educate.* CMI Press.

serious harm. And, how could they not? Each vaccine contains numerous toxic ingredients. We are not injecting these toxic ingredients into adults with developed immune systems - which would still be extremely risky - but into tiny babies with immature immune systems.

At this point in my research, I was aware that:

1) Vaccines did not cause diseases to decline; they were already declining.

2) Most diseases vaccinated against would not be deadly or serious if contracted today.

3) Vaccines contain numerous toxic ingredients at levels above what the FDA has approved for food additives and over the counter medications.

4) Chronic conditions and serious/deadly diseases have risen in proportion to the rise in the number of vaccination programs and in areas with aggressive vaccination campaigns.

Follow the Money

Vaccines are enormously profitable for drug companies. They are enormously profitable for medical professionals. And they are enormously profitable for the major stockholders in drug companies. Many, many people make lots and lots of money from vaccines. That's not necessarily a bad thing. However, whenever there is a lot of money involved, there exists the potential for abuse, deception, and hidden agendas.

Recent U.S. legislation has exempted lawsuits against pharmaceutical firms in the event of adverse reactions to vaccines, which are very common. Once a vaccine is mandated, the vaccine manufacturer is no longer liable for adverse reactions. So drug companies can make vaccines, and do so risk-free. If a vaccine is dangerous or doesn't work or causes adverse reactions or even death, the drug company continues to make a profit on it; there are no risks or repercussions for turning out bad vaccines. Pharmaceutical companies, like all publicly held companies, exist to maximize shareholder wealth. That isn't necessarily good or bad; it just is, so it needs to be factored in. In addition, vaccinations are the bread and butter of any pediatric practice. Routine immunizations bring parents back for multiple office visits. Without vaccinations, the need for pediatricians would plunge.

Doctors may or may not be aware of the facts surrounding vaccinations. Most doctors don't have a few hours a day to research vaccines, which is required to really dissect all available information and begin to ask relevant questions about the data and follow it through. Some doctors may be aware of the facts. However, because the facts go against what they learned in medical school and have been repeated over and over by the CDC, they purposely don't look too closely at the data. After all, no good can come of it. If they look under the covers, there is no going back; they must make a difficult decision. Do they keep on keeping on, knowing the harm they are bringing, or do they take a stand and risk their practice and financial future? Neither is appealing. Sometimes it's easier to just not look too closely.

From a profitability standpoint, here are the questions I asked myself:

1. If I don't vaccinate, does anyone profit? No, they do not.

2. If I choose to vaccinate, does anyone profit from that? Absolutely! Pharmaceutical companies, pediatricians, shareholders, and many others.

3. If we assume that vaccines increase the chance for future diseases, does anyone profit from that? Definitely. The entire medical industry needs sick people in order to stay in business. Researchers and drug companies also profit from diseases such as cancer, asthma, immune disorders. These diseases require a lot of research and drug usage.

4. If I don't vaccinate - and if many others choose not to vaccinate - does anyone *lose* money? Yes, everyone loses money if I don't vaccinate - from the drug companies, to the pediatrician's, to the entire healthcare industry.

Nobody makes money from convincing people *not* to vaccinate. Many will lose money if more and more people choose not to vaccinate. If pharmaceutical companies lose profits then stock values decline and that will impact anyone with a 401K or a 529 account or a brokerage account, or other type of investment.

Summary

Consider this question: do you believe that the scientists working for the CDC on vaccines actually vaccinate their own children? Most people openly admit that they don't believe the high ranking populous – the people who are "in the know" about the ingredients in vaccines - ever vaccinate their children. But, while most will concede that it's doubtful "those in the know" vaccinate their own children, these same people choose to vaccinate their own children for reasons they can't articulate. They don't trust their own knowledge, intuition, opinions and feelings on the topic. After all, how can they be right when *everyone* is doing it? Much of what lies behind this has to do with a person's upbringing and schooling, which you will read more about in the Homeschooling section of this book.

Throughout my research, I wanted nothing more than to pretend I didn't stumble upon the information, and would have loved to put the cork back in the bottle. There is nothing remotely comfortable about this type of information. Discovering it opens the door to possibilities many people never dreamed of and *awakens* something that feels unfamiliar and scary. Even if I chose to block out the bigger picture and what it means about the people and institutions in power and humanity in general, I was still in a position to have to make some difficult decisions. It is *easier* being ignorant and living in the dark. Why couldn't I just meander along, half-awake like so many others? How easy it would have been to just do what everyone else was doing and keep my eyes tightly closed.

It's comforting to believe that "everyone" has your best interests at heart and that "they" wouldn't lead you down the wrong path. But, as you get wiser (and usually a bit older as well) you soon realize that "everyone" is really just made up of a single individual plus another, plus another, plus another. Just because they are all grouped together forming a department of the government or a committee doesn't mean that group will not mislead you, will not follow their own agenda at your expense and will not tell half-truths or even lies to turn a profit.

Let me ask you this. If one of your friends were to tell you that injecting toxins into yourself and your family members was a good idea, would you believe him? Maybe you would if it was a good friend. But, what if your good friend stood to make a ton of money if you believed him – would that make his claims more or less credible to you? What if all of your neighbors were trying to convince you to inject the toxins? Would the group mentality get to you and convince you not to think for yourself? If your neighbors would become rich by convincing you, would their claims become more or less valid to you? Think about this: in these scenarios, you *know* these people. Even if they would become rich by convincing you to go along, you might be inclined, at least, to listen to them because they are your friends. In the world of vaccines, you don't know the people who are getting rich off convincing you to inject toxic chemicals into your babies. Does that make it more or less likely that they won't be looking out for your best interests?

If someone asked you to inject yourself right now with mercury mixed with other toxic ingredients, would you do it? How about if they told you it *might* prevent you from getting an infectious disease that you won't likely get anyway because it's relatively rare? Would you do it then? What if they then told you that even if you did contract this somewhat rare disease, it would be unlikely to cause serious harm? Would you then think it worthwhile to inject yourself with mercury and other toxins? What if I added to all of this, that if you do inject yourself, you would be seriously inhibiting your immune system for the rest of your life? Would that make a difference to you? What about if you were asked to inject a toxic concoction into your child's body. Does that make it easier or harder to say "yes" to this request? Would it sweeten the pot at all if I told you that hundreds of thousands of people will make a lot of money if you go ahead and inject yourself or your child? Would that make the injection more appealing or less appealing? What if I told you that all of those people and companies will lose a *lot* of money if you don't inject yourself? Are you more or less likely to take the injection?

Here's something else to think about. Under what circumstances *would* you agree to the injection? What if it would *absolutely* prevent the disease? It's still a somewhat rare disease that could be cured if you contracted it and you'd still be injecting toxins into your body and damaging your immune system. So, even if you *knew* the injection would prohibit you from getting the disease, would it be worth it? In the real world of vaccines, we have no proof that they prevent the acquisition of any disease. In fact, we have proof that they bring on diseases and in many cases the very disease they were meant to prevent.

Here are the circumstances that would have to be true in order for me to inject myself with mercury, formaldehyde, aluminum and other toxins:

1. The injection would have to prevent a disease so hideous, that if I were to contract it, it would mean an immediate start to a very painful death.

2. I would have to be fairly certain that without the injection, I would most likely contract the hideous disease.

3. The injection would have to protect me for my entire life.

4. The injection must have no negative impact at all on my body or health.

To inject this into my baby, all of the above would have to be true, *plus*, I would have to have concrete, indisputable evidence of the above, along with no possibility of finding contrary evidence.

Let's be realistic here. Even if we dismiss every study we have ever read about the vaccine ingredients causing harm, you are still left with the fact that the infectious diseases were retreating long before vaccines were introduced, and there is no proof that vaccines prevent any disease. We know on some level that pumping an infant's body full of formaldehyde and other toxins will have serious adverse effects in the short and long term. We even know that living too close to molds and radioactivity causes serious harm – that's just living *near* them, not injecting them. If this entire vaccine debacle were to play out on a TV show, the plot would seem so implausible that the show would be canceled.

Based on what I've written here, you may be thinking that I probably decided not to vaccinate. But you would be wrong. I never decided *not* to vaccinate. The decision I made was this: I decided to allow my daughter to keep her immune cells and system healthy and uncontaminated with toxic chemicals. I decided to allow my daughter the chance to gain natural, lifelong immunity to enable her maximum fighting power against infectious diseases and immune related disorders and illnesses. So, I did not make the negative decision to not vaccinate. I made the positive decision in favor of a strong immune system and overall health. There is a fine but distinct difference there.

I didn't even dream it would be so good. But I would never let my children come close to the thing. Vladimir Zworykin, aged 92 on his invention, the television.

TV-Free

When I was pregnant with Genevieve, I envisioned buying videos like the Baby Einstein series, and having her watch educational TV shows like Sesame Street. So, I stocked up on videos months before I gave birth. When my baby was born, however, she was rarely awake, which was only natural. She mostly slept and ate. As she grew older and stayed awake longer, I began to interact with her and watch her interact with her environment. I enjoyed watching her grow and change, focusing on objects, reaching for something new, and making connections within the world around her.

As she neared her first birthday, I realized that she had not watched TV or seen a movie or a commercial. In fact, when she was awake, everything was so fascinating and new that the thought of turning on the TV or popping in a movie never occurred to me. There was so much to do and see – for both of us.

When my friend's kids were between the ages of 1 and 3, they often asked me about what TV shows Genevieve liked or what movies she had seen. She, however, was only a year old and there was just no time for that. She had so much to see and touch and investigate. When she was awake, I didn't want to waste any of our time on peripheral things, when we could be interacting with each other, with other people, and with our environments. I began to feel a little guilty – maybe I should try to fit in some TV time for her. After all, I always thought I would give her a "head start" in life by showing her educational videos and TV shows.

I honestly set out to try and find time to fit in a movie or a TV show to see if she was interested. But, we never could seem to find the time; she was just so engaged in her surroundings. It almost seemed like a shame to disconnect her from her world so that she could passively watch something on TV. We barely had enough time for all of her active pursuits.

As Genevieve neared her second birthday, many of my friends would talk about how horrible it was to take their two-year-olds grocery shopping. They would throw tantrums because they wanted certain cereals and toys and candy bars. I couldn't relate to any of that. Because Genevieve had never watched TV or seen a commercial, she had no idea what cereals she *should* want or what toys she *should* enjoy or what candy bars she *should* like. She just rode in the cart and helped me put things in. Nothing in the grocery store looked familiar to her, with the exception of the things we regularly bought.

In addition, because she didn't see TV, she had no idea what McDonald's was or any other fast food restaurant. I was never one to go to fast food restaurants before she was born so after she was born, I never had any reason to go there. But, many of my friend's kids knew all about McDonald's through TV commercials. They had to drive certain routes to avoid passing the restaurant or their child would scream to go there.

Genevieve had no idea that kids ate cereal for breakfast and not broccoli, which made it easy for me to continue feeding her vegetables for breakfast. (It was easier to have her eat her veggies at breakfast since that's when she was hungriest and less likely to put up a fight). She had no idea that kids were supposed to be watching lots of TVs and missed out on being bombarded with commercials for toys, candy, gum, and medications. She had no idea that going to McDonald's would make her deliriously happy (I'm not sure why, but the kids in the commercials seem incredibly happy about being there. Certainly, they are not yet aware of the obesity epidemic).

However, when Genevieve was about three, we were having particularly bad weather and I turned on the TV to see the news while she was awake and in the room – something I'd never ever done before. A commercial was on and there were kids playing with a toy, looking happy and excited. She turned to us and said something like "I want that toy – those kids really like it!" It was very clear that the reaction of the kids on the TV resonated with her. She assumed that the toy was making them super happy and that if she got the toy, she would feel the same way. *Of course* she would think this way! That was the whole intent.

I immediately turned off the TV. I did not want her artificially desiring some object, thinking that it would make her as happy as the kids on the commercial appeared to be. Even worse, what if we bought her the toy and she didn't feel as happy? Would she feel sad and wonder if something was missing or something was wrong with her?

A few months later, a toy catalog came to the house and there was a girl on the cover playing with a doll and the doll was riding a horse. Genevieve mentioned that she wanted that toy for

Christmas and when I asked her what she liked about it she said, "The girl in the picture seems to really like it and is smiling". Of course, I took advantage of that opportunity to explain to her what she was seeing. With TV, the images come together so quickly and then move on to the next thing; there isn't time to explain it all. At least with print ads, we can look at a picture and discuss it for as long as we need to.

My typical TV watching habits have always gone like this: If there was a show I wanted to watch, I'd turn the TV on to watch the show, and then turn it off after the show. I wasn't familiar with the type of environment where the TV was always turned on as "background" noise. Until Genevieve was about two and ½, I never made the conscious decision to leave the TV off while she was awake. It was just never on because there was nothing that I wanted to watch while she was awake. In other words, being actively engaged with Genevieve was always more important than being passively engaged watching someone else live their pseudo life.

Soon after, I finally made a formal policy out of what I'd been informally practicing. I decided to allow her to fully engage in her life in an active way, creating her own interests and entertainment. I also decided to let her develop and form her own opinions about foods that she liked, toys that were interesting, and clothes that she thought looked nice, without seeing how others felt about those things. I decided to allow myself the opportunity to be her main influence, uncontested and without contradiction. This meant that the TV would not be on when she was awake. Raising her according to my standards was very important to me. The last thing I needed was someone else coming into my home and contradicting everything I was trying to teach her, and undermining her own opinions.

TV-Free

As I was making the decision about TV, I began researching all available data about the impact of TV, commercials, and passive entertainment on children. In addition, I began looking into the value of being actively engaged in one's life as a child, and creating entertainment and interests without suggestion from media and adults. With this particular issue, it didn't matter if commercials and TV had no negative impact on children. All impacts could have been positive and I would have still valued active engagement with people and the environment as more beneficial than any form of passive entertainment. Below is a small sampling of the TV data I found during the course of my research (see the References section at the end of this book for information on source data).

- In an average U.S. home, the TV is on for 6 hours and 47 minutes every day.[32]

- The average child watches television 28 hours per week. [32]

- Sixty-six percent (66%) of Americans regularly watch television while eating dinner.[32]

- Forty-nine percent (49%) of Americans say they watch too much TV.[32]

- Parents report that they spend an average of 3.5 minutes in *meaningful* conversation with their children.[32]

---

[32] A. C. Nielsen Company.
http://www.csun.edu/science/health/docs/tv&health.html

- Seventy percent (70%) of day care centers in the U.S. have children watch TV during the day.[33]

- Seventy-three percent (73%) of parents say they would like to limit their children's TV watching.[33]

- When 4-6 year olds were asked if they'd rather spend time with their fathers or watch TV, 54 percent preferred watching TV.[33]

- American children spend an average of 900 hours per year in school and 1500 hours watching television.

- The average U.S. child sees 20,000 30-second TV commercials per year.[33]

- When surveyed (in 1993), 92 percent of parents said that TV commercials make children *too* materialistic.[33]

- When surveyed, children said their favorite commercials were those for food products and fast-food restaurants. Children see 300 junk food commercials per week on average.[34]

- In 1993, the top 100 leading TV advertisers spent a combined $15 billion.[34]

---

[33] A. C. Nielsen Company.
http://www.csun.edu/science/health/docs/tv&health.html
[34] Linn, S. (2004). *Consuming Kids: Protecting our children from the onslaught of marketing & advertising.* New York: Anchor Books

- By the time the average child finishes elementary school, they have seen 8,000 murders on TV. They have seen 200,000 by the time they are 18.[35]

- Seventy-nine percent (79%) of Americans believe TV violence helps create real life mayhem.[35]

- A recent (2009) New York Times poll revealed that Americans have a starkly negative view of popular culture, and blame television more than any other factor for teenage sex and violence. Most parents saw a direct connection between popular culture and behavior, noting that their children imitate the behavior and language they picked up from television, movies and radio. Most felt powerless to prevent their children from seeing or hearing inappropriate entertainment.[36]

The American Academy of Pediatrics has an official statement about TV and children under the age of two and that statement is – don't do it![37] These early years are crucial in a child's development. The Academy is concerned about the impact of television programming intended for younger children. Pediatricians strongly oppose targeted programming, especially when it's used to market toys, games, dolls, unhealthy food and other products to toddlers. Any positive effect of television on

---

[35] A. C. Nielsen Company.
http://www.csun.edu/science/health/docs/tv&health.html
[36] Federal Communications Commission (FCC).
http://www.fcc.gov/Speeches/Hundt/spreh522.txt
[37] American Academy of Pediatrics (AAP).
http://www.aap.org/sections/media/toddlerstv.htm

infants and toddlers is still open to question, but the benefits of parent-child interactions are proven. Under age two, talking, singing, reading, listening to music or playing are far more important to a child's development than any TV show, regardless of the educational content.

Dr. Dimitri A. Christakis, lead researcher and director of the Child Health Institute at Children's Hospital and Regional Medical Center, Seattle, Washington, has said that TV watching "rewires" an infant's brain. The damage shows up at age seven when children have difficulty paying attention in school. Dr. Christakis's research also shows that exposing a baby's developing brain to TV may cause permanent changes in developing neural pathways. A study from the American Academy of Pediatrics shows that watching TV as a toddler is correlated to developing Attention Deficit Hyperactivity Disorder (ADHD) later in life.[38]

The American Academy of Pediatrics has said that too much screen time is linked to obesity in children, irregular sleep patterns, behavioral problems, impaired academic performance, and less time for creative play. In one study of children from 3rd to 8th grade, the results showed that those who watched more TV experienced more anxiety and depression, as well as more post-traumatic stress disorder. When young children watch TV, they think abstractly rather than concretely and are unable to fully separate fiction from reality. This results in more fears and anxiety.[39]

---

[38] Dr. Dimitri Christakis, Seattle Children's Hospital. http://www.seattlechildrens.org/about/stories/harnessing-technology-for-the-benefit-of-children/
[39] American Academy of Pediatrics (AAP). http://www.aap.org/sections/media/toddlerstv.htm

Eating Habits

Many studies have shown that children under the age of six believe that commercials tell the truth.[40] Children rely on what the announcer is saying and when in stores, will request what they recall being told to buy (in the commercial). Ads for junk food have been shown to have the greatest impact on increasing a child's caloric consumption.

I am responsible for my daughter's eating habits. Until she is old enough to earn her own money, drive herself to the grocery store, and buy the food she wants, then I am solely responsible for what she eats. If she overeats, it's my fault. If she eats too much junk food, it's my fault. If she eats fruits and vegetables each day, it's because of me. I can't point a finger at anyone else: It's my responsibility and I know it. As a child, she has absolutely no power to control her own food. Oh sure, parents will say their children "won't" eat vegetables, or their children "make them" buy sugary cereals. That's a very convenient way of absolving themselves of their responsibility and accountability. I hear parents say things like, "I know Billy is way too heavy but I just can't get him to eat anything except cookies and crackers". Really? Could that possibly be true? If you didn't buy cookies or crackers, how could he eat them? If you were to only buy healthy food, would he allow himself to starve? Of course not.

Because it is *my* responsibility to keep my child safe and healthy, then it is up to me to be the primary influence over what she eats. I model proper eating habits by eating mainly healthy food in front of Genevieve, and buying/preparing only healthy

[40] Linn, S. (2004). *Consuming Kids: Protecting our children from the onslaught of marketing & advertising.* New York: Anchor Books

food for her. It's always been that way. She sees me do it and then wants to do it herself. I buy mostly healthy food and have guidelines around the number of sweets we have per week – and we have them together. She is well aware that a vegetable should be eaten with every meal, and she's well versed on other healthy eating habits. She is also aware that she must "move her body" and get exercise each day. This is my duty as a parent; no one else has this responsibility.

I've often asked myself this question: Would I allow people I don't know to come into my home 300 times per week and show Genevieve junk food and talk about how great it tastes? Would I allow them to bring giggling children, eating junk food, into my house? That is exactly what I'd be doing if I allowed her to watch TV. If she was a typical child, she'd be watching 28 hours of TV per week and seeing 300 junk food ads – all of which she'd believe are the truth. Doing that would absolutely undermine everything I've been doing and make it impossible for me to do my job as a parent. Worse yet, it would make it very difficult for her to develop healthy eating habits that would help her live her life to the fullest.

Here are some excerpts from studies and data available regarding nutrition and TV:

- In the 1960s approximately 5 percent of children between the ages of 6 and 17 were severely overweight. In 1995, 11 percent of this age group is severely overweight. The main culprits were found to be inactivity due to the doubling of TV watching hours, and a high-calorie diet.[41]

---

[41] Anderson, P.M., Butcher, K. F. (2006). *Childhood obesity: Trends and potential causes*. Dartmouth College.

- According to pediatricians, the easiest way to increase activity is to turn off the TV. Everything else (other than sleeping) uses more energy than watching TV.[42]

- The American Academy of Pediatrics states that watching TV is linked to obesity (in children who watch more than 2 hours per day), and less play time.[43]

- A 2005 Institute of Medicine report stated that there is strong evidence that television advertising of foods and beverages has a direct influence on what children choose to eat. Food advertising can make children crave junk food.[44]

- The report also found that the dominant focus of food and beverage marketing to children and youth is for products high in calories and low in nutrients, and this is sharply out of balance with healthy diets.[44]

- Of food ads that target children, 34 percent are for candy and snacks, 29 percent are for cereal, 10 percent are for beverages, 10 percent are for fast-food, 4 percent are for dairy products, 4 percent are for prepared food and the rest are for breads and pastries and dine-in restaurants.[45]

---

[42] http://www.turnoffyourtv.com/healtheducation/junkfood.html
[43] American Academy of Pediatrics (AAP).
http://www.aap.org/sections/media/toddlerstv.htm
[44] Federal Communications Commission (FCC).
www.fcc.gov/obesity/march07meeting/Gootman.pdf
[45] Federal Trade Commission (FTC). Marketing Food to Children and Adolescents.
www.ftc.gov/os/2008/07/P064504**food**mktingreportappendices.pdf

Obviously, I can't keep my daughter safe and healthy and still allow her to watch TV, knowing what I know about the negative impacts. Choosing to allow TV would be the same as blatantly stating that I relinquish my control over her eating habits and have decided not to be accountable for her health or weight.

Materialism

It's always been very important to me that Genevieve not spend her life chasing "things". It's fine if she ends up being upper middle class or even wealthy as an adult, as long as she doesn't get her sense of self-worth from the things she accumulates. I spend a lot of time talking to her about the importance of not being wasteful, and the benefits of giving to people in need. Things will come and go and if she derives a significant amount of her identity and self-worth from having and displaying her things then she will never be truly happy. Someone will always have more and she'll constantly be measuring herself against what other people have. If she loses her things in a natural disaster like a tornado, then she'll be completely devastated. I want her to be secure and happy with herself from an internal perspective and not an external one. I don't want her self-worth to be measured by what things she has relative to what other's have.

Television plays a major role in building materialism. In a 2002 study, it was found that people who watch a lot of TV are much more materialistic than those who don't. Television portrays wealth very positively. Researchers have shown that the world of television is much more affluent than the real world. There are very few programs that feature poor people and the ones that do, don't portray them positively. Many studies have shown that the more people watch TV, the more materialistic they are. The same has been found to be true of violence, by the way.[46]

---

[46] Linn, S. (2004). *Consuming Kids: Protecting our children from the onslaught of marketing & advertising.* New York: Anchor Books

Unvaccinated, Homeschooled, and TV-Free

The average American will spend 15 percent of their waking hours watching TV, with its huge houses, fancy cars and unlimited consumption. Images portrayed on television are exaggerated, and heavy TV viewers get a distorted view of the world. These people believe that most of the world is wealthier than they actually are. This leads them to believe they aren't living the way they should – the way the "majority" of others are living - so they begin to consume more and more in an effort to fit in. But they aren't trying to fit in with reality – they are trying to fit in with fiction. Their neighbors are doing the same thing. When people find that they can't have everything that the families on TV have, they can become unhappy and depressed.

Several studies have confirmed that the people who watch the most TV are the least satisfied with their lives, while the people who watch the least amount of TV are the most satisfied with their lives.[47]

But it's not just TV shows that glamorize consumption and wealth, it's also commercials. Children pay attention to commercials as if they were watching television shows. Kids make up a huge portion of consumer spending, and according to a study at Texas A&M University, they spend $8-$14 billion per year. Company executives are well aware of this and advertise relentlessly during children's programs.

It's important to me that my daughter has a true sense of internal happiness that won't be diminished if she compares what she has to what other's have (or what she *thinks* others have). Watching TV is something that would work against this goal.

---

[47] Linn, S. (2004). *Consuming Kids: Protecting our children from the onslaught of marketing & advertising.* New York: Anchor Books

Summary

There's no denying that television is an enjoyable activity, no matter how old you are. However, it's important to understand that television doesn't exist to entertain anyone. *Television exists to make profits* – profits for advertisers, profits for networks, profits for shareholders, etc. Nobody makes any money at all if no one watches TV; in fact, money will be lost if more people stop watching TV. When we watch TV, we (adults) understand the profit motives and filter the information accordingly. But, children do not fully understand the purpose of TV and they can't properly position the messages and images. Television marketing directed to children is exploitative. Advertisers want to build brand awareness and brand loyalty. Young children do not have the cognitive ability to understand the persuasive intent of advertising.

Here are some fun quotes about television:

- If you came home and you found a strange man teaching your kids to punch each other, or trying to sell them all kinds of products, you'd kick him right out of the house, but here you are; you come in and the TV is on, and you don't think twice about it. (Jerome Singer).

- Television is an invention that permits you to be entertained in your living room by people you wouldn't have in your home. (David Frost).

- I have prevented my kids from watching MTV at home. It's not safe for kids. (Tom Freston, former president of MTV).

- Television has proved that people will look at anything rather than each other. (Ann Landers).

- Kids don't choose television over people; they choose television because of lack of people interaction. (Brook Noel).

- Television keeps the masses occupied. What if everyone decided they wanted to make something of their lives? Television keeps the competition down and keeps criminals off the street. What if everyone decided to go to law school or medical school? It would sure make it tough on the rest of us. (Jim Urbanovich).

- If the television craze continues with the present level of programs, we are destined to have a nation of morons. (Daniel Marsh, 1950).

According to a Rutgers University psychologist, millions of Americans are so hooked on television that they fit the criteria for substance abuse as defined in the official psychiatric manual. Virtually all independent scholars agree that there is evidence that television can cause aggressive behavior. Since my daughter is only five, I have not fully researched the violence angle. I won't need to though. There are so many other reasons why she won't be watching TV that violence will never get to be a concern of mine.

While this information is all very interesting and informative, I decided that Genevieve wouldn't be watching TV without taking any of this information into consideration. The decision was made long before I began fully researching the impact of television. I actually never decided *not* to allow her to watch TV. Instead, my decision was to allow her maximum time to interact and engage with her environment. I decided to allow her to learn through doing and being rather than by watching. I decided to allow her to form her own opinions about what looks good and what's fun to play with, rather than having television programs and commercials attempt to decide it for her. I decided to teach her that human interaction and interaction with her environment in the "here and now" is of the utmost importance.

So far, the results are good. She has never once said she's bored; she has no idea what that means. She's used to finding her own entertainment and would never expect that someone else would find it for her. She is knowledgeable about all of the popular "television" characters such as Dora and Barney through the books we get at the library. I make sure she gets books that familiarize her with these characters so that she can talk the same language as her friends. She's slim and active, the way children should be. And, she knows the value of healthy eating and regular exercise. I honestly don't know where TV would fit into our lives and what could possibly be gained from it!

An eternal question about children is, how should we educate them? Politicians and educators consider more school days in a year, more science and math, the use of computers and other technology in the classroom, more exams and tests, more certification for teachers, and less money for art. All of these responses come from the place where we want to make the child into the best adult possible, not in the ancient Greek sense of virtuous and wise, but in the sense of one who is an efficient part of the machinery of society. But on all these counts, soul is neglected. Thomas Moore

Homeschool

If you asked me in my 20s or 30s if I would ever consider homeschooling my children I would have wondered how I could possibly know someone who would ask such an inane question. Throughout adulthood, I have thought and said things like "Children should be in school year-round"; "Children have way too much free time on their hands"; "We are falling behind the rest of the world in education because our children don't spend enough time in school and don't get nearly enough homework; "The best schools are the ones with the most stringent rules"; "Why are schools wasting time on gym, playtime and art classes when they could be using the time for more math and science?"

Why wouldn't I have thought those things? As a child, I was a very obedient student who usually received top grades. I went on to get a Bachelor's degree, two Master's degrees and a Ph.D. Formal education is a way of life for me. And, by most standards, I could be considered successful or even very successful.

As far back as I can remember, my parents and other well meaning adults said things like "I hope you like cleaning toilets because that's what you'll be doing for the rest of your life if you don't go to school", or "if you don't go to school you'll end up in the gutter". These kinds of sentiments let me know there are certain roles people can play that are bad, undesirable, or unacceptable. However, these pointed comments *never* recognized *happiness* as important or relevant. Realistically, if a person cleans toilets, enjoys it and is a very happy person, that is a good thing. And, if a person is "in the gutter" it may not have anything to do with their schooling.

It was made crystal clear that going to school and getting good grades were the most important things in life – it's what *life was about.* Nothing mattered unless and until you had successfully completed at least twelve years of school. So, as a child, I went about the business of childhood which was going to school and trying to get good grades. I never questioned this just like I never questioned the importance of eating food, or brushing my teeth. It just had to be.

As a young adult, I never questioned the importance of school. After all, I had a successful career; I was financially successful and socially successful. When I saw children acting like.....well.....*children*.......I would shake my head and mutter "Shouldn't they be in school?" Or, "Apparently, they don't have enough homework to keep them busy." If I never had children, I would probably still be thinking this way today. There wouldn't likely have been any life-changing event to make me question my views.

When I was pregnant with Genevieve, I started looking into "the best schools" in my area; the schools with the longest days, the schools that started teaching calculus before the other schools did; the schools that had year-round schedules; the schools where the children had to be able to read prior to entering kindergarten. There was no question about it: I had the means and the ability so my daughter was going to get the best education available.

Now, I should say that at the time I had Genevieve, I was in the middle of my Ph.D. program and getting a Ph.D. is all about research. During the course of any research degree, you learn how to dissect research done by other people. You read studies and their conclusions and you learn to question every sentence, and pick apart any conclusion and find hidden agendas, while poking holes in findings. So, at the time of Genevieve's birth, I was starting to question studies, mainstream opinion, and my own strongly held beliefs and value systems about what constituted an exemplary education.

I was thirty-eight when I had Genevieve. She was important enough to me that I didn't want to cut corners. I drew upon all of my experience, knowledge, intuition, and feelings when making decisions for and about her. There was no decision that was too minor to spend time researching and thinking through.

With regard to schooling, I spent most of my time trying to find "the best" school based on my long-held beliefs about what good schools were, up until Genevieve was almost two-years-old. Around that time I started to veer a bit off track into alternative schooling methods and options. But, that whole arena felt forbidden to me and it took me quite a bit of time to look at it objectively. Nonetheless, I overcame my own objections and shortly before Genevieve turned three I was committed to homeschooling.

There are many methods of homeschooling and the method I selected is called unschooling. This is very different from traditional homeschools whereby "school" is set up at home, complete with curriculum, grades, tests, and external rewards for behaviors and achievement. The unschooling method is at the opposite end of the spectrum; it is entirely child-led and child-directed with no curriculum, tests, or grades.

Whenever someone asks me why I'm unschooling my daughter, I'm at a complete loss for words. I can either give a vague, one-sentence answer, or I can ask the person to take the next week off of work and we'll go sit in a coffee shop for the week while I explain my reasons. I usually opt for the first choice because most people who ask don't *really* want to know. In my experience, many people who ask the question are feeling defensive. They feel that because I've chosen to homeschool, I must be negatively judging them for sending their kids to "regular" school. And, I've seen that they ask me for my reasons in order to discredit them in their own minds, thereby confirming their own choices. However, I'm not really concerned with what other people are doing with their kids. My mind is solely focused on my own daughter and my choices for her and we all have the freedom to do what we feel is best for our children.

There are many, many reasons why I've decided to homeschool using the unschooling method. I'm presenting my top ten reasons here. Of these, not one of them has anything to do with *what* is taught in schools. Nor do they have anything to do with religious views, political views, school violence or accelerating the learning process. I mention this because whenever I state that I'm homeschooling, people say things like "Ohhhhhhh, I didn't realize you were *so* religious" (which I'm not), or "I heard more people are homeschooling these days because of all the school shootings and violence", or "What school subjects do you disagree with?", or "Are you sure you want Genevieve to get *that* far ahead of other kids her age – won't she feel *different*?"

Homeschool

There seem to be commonly held stereotypes about homeschooling families as well as assumptions around the reasons why people homeschool. None of these assumptions have anything to do with *my* top ten reasons (or my top twenty reasons). In addition, I'm not a survivalist with a stock-pile of weapons, we don't live on a commune (and I have no intention of sewing Genevieve denim jumpers in a variety of colors).

Reason 1: Children are Whole at Every Age

Childhood is not preparation for adulthood - it is a part of life.
A. Neill

I'm just going to come right out and say it. Much of my childhood was wasted because I was in school for six to eight hours a day for twelve straight years. The reason I say that it was wasted is because it was spent, almost entirely, in preparation for *becoming* something. Now, I'm not against preparation. In fact, I'm a project manager, so my life revolves around planning, preparation and process. What I *am* against is devaluing the days and moments of childhood and placing primary importance on preparation for adulthood.

Children are not "adults in waiting." Yes, we need to teach them the skills, knowledge, and behaviors that are most likely to help them have well-adjusted lives as adults. But, does that process really have to take seventy-five percent of their daily focus for twelve years? Does that process require that we devalue their childhood and devalue their opinions about what they want to do with their time? Does that process have to mean that they trade their daily happiness for preparation?

One question that I hoped Genevieve would never be asked is, "What do you want to be when you grow up?" Genevieve is five years old and already I've heard people ask her that question. What answer do people hope to get? Why would we ask *what* do you want to be when you grow up? The word "what" implies the child will turn into an inanimate object. Do we expect a child to say, "I'd like to be a dining room table when I grow up", or "I want to be a fishing pole when I grow up?" A child is whole and complete as they are, in this very moment. They don't need to *be* anything or *become* anything. They

76

already *are* something – they are children. School leads children to believe there are predefined professions and opportunities available and that they must select one and do A, B, and C in order to achieve it. That is completely false and robs children of their ability to dream up their own goals and imagine what their own future looks like on their terms. If children believe, from an early age, that they have to select from a list of existing professions, then what chance do they have to actually create their own new profession, or find a way to make a living doing something they love? Children are born to create, which is all that life is about. Creating.

Children aren't striving to become whole. Children are whole, every day and at every age. Their opinions count every day and at every age. Schooling makes children believe they aren't yet whole and their opinions don't count and they don't yet fully matter as human beings. Why does schooling make them believe this? Because every day is spent preparing, preparing, preparing. They prepare for quizzes, and they prepare for tests, and they prepare for grades, and they prepare for moving to the next grade, and they prepare for moving to the next school. All of their time is *future* focused. We teach them that the *present* does not matter at all. So, they prepare, and prepare, and prepare. Preparing becomes a way of life. So much so, they don't even stop to think about it anymore; it's just the way things are meant to be. Prepare, and prepare, and prepare. Only the future matters. Children aren't good enough today. But they will be tomorrow, next year, three years from now, twelve years from now…

And, of course, the future never arrives. The future is tomorrow but then when tomorrow comes, you spend almost all of it preparing for the next day. And then the future is next year, but you spend all of next year preparing for the following year. Soon enough, you have a lifestyle focused on the future, devaluing your *moments* – your *nows*. And, what is all of this preparation for? Supposedly, it is so that you *can* enjoy your moments. The idea is if you spend enough time preparing, you'll get to a point where you can take in a deep breath and start appreciating your moments. But, how could that possibly ever happen? You've never learned that moments count and that *now* matters. So, even when you are done with school, you are so future-focused that you then prepare for the next thing and then for the next thing.

There is an old saying: "Life is what happens while you are preparing to live". *So, if you aren't enjoying your preparation then you aren't enjoying your life.*

Here is another popular saying: First I was dying to finish high school and start college. And then, I was dying to finish college and start working. And then, I was dying to marry and have children. And, then I was dying for my children to grow old enough for school so I could return to work. And then, I was dying to retire. And now, I'm just dying. And suddenly, I realize, I forgot to live.

Children have as much to teach adults as we have to teach them. They have arrived in the present and they are whole exactly as they are now. Rather than keeping them focused on busy work, with the intent of preparing them for the future, let them live and experience and teach and grow today, and in this moment, and in this moment, and in this one. After all, don't they naturally have what we are all striving for?

Before school starts for children, they are happy and playful just about every day. They choose their own activities, they choose what they want to learn next, they laugh and appreciate each moment. This is what we work hard to obtain – the opportunity to relax and enjoy our moments. Didn't we go through years of school so that we could enjoy our moments? So, children already *have* something that we all want. They have the freedom to choose their activities and enjoy their moments. There is no other reason why we all work, except to enjoy our moments *today*. That is exactly what children already do. But, then we take this away from them. We train them to focus on the future and forget about their moments.

This is not to say that we shouldn't have them prepare for the future. But, does their preparation have to be nearly all-consuming, and done in a way that completely disregards their present moment awareness, forcing them to sacrifice their todays for their tomorrows? Can't the preparation be enjoyable and self-directed? If every "today" is spent planning and preparing then tomorrow never actually comes. And if it does, how will they know *it* has arrived? And, when *it* arrives, will they then suddenly be able to stop the planning cycle and just enjoy? Not likely.

I want Genevieve to live fully now, today. And, I want her to be prepared for the future as well. But, I never want her to sacrifice her todays for her tomorrows. There is a way to meet both goals.

By homeschooling, I'm able to encourage her enjoyment of the vast majority of her moments, while sprinkling in the amount of preparation that will help her to be successful as an adult. I am able to teach her to focus on what she has here and now. If she's happy right now, then she's happy forever because now is all she has – it is her forever. In reality, if she's happy now, then she has achieved her goals and *all* of our goals as well. That's what all of this preparing is for, right? To achieve happiness. And, she's there. Do you think that if she's already achieved her goals today, right now, that she cannot possibly be happy in the future because she won't be adequately prepared? Or, is it more likely that because she's learned that moments count, and she's learned what makes her moments happy ones, that she'll likely continue that trend in her future, creating situations that meet her criteria for happiness?

Genevieve is happy and joyful everyday. She discovers new things, and learns new things everyday. And, all of her days will continue to be that way; there is no reason why that would ever end. The only way that it will end is if she suddenly starts to believe that moments don't count and that she's not whole as she is now, and then embarks on a daily ritual of preparing and planning and preparing and planning, thereby reinforcing every day that she is not of value until.....until.....until......and starts chasing a future that she isn't sure will come and won't be able to identify even if it does come.

Genevieve is whole at her current age. Her happiness counts today. Her opinions are important right now. The last thing I would every consider doing is putting her into school where she prepares endlessly and is made to believe she is incomplete now and she must learn from adults rather than teach adults *as well as learn from them*. I want her to set goals and learn what it takes to achieve those goals. However, achieving the goal should never be more important than what she is experiencing in the moment. Achieving a goal should never be so important that she decides to be unhappy through most of the process required to meet the goal. If she doesn't enjoy the preparation daily, and in the moment, then achieving the goal will never be worth giving up all of her "nows".

Homeschooling allows me to let Genevieve enjoy most of her daily hours, in any way that she chooses. This is because homeschooling only takes a fraction of the time traditional schooling takes to impart the same amount of information. Every hour of traditional classroom learning is equivalent to ten to fifteen minutes of homeschooling, if a child is taught by someone who knows him intimately (what motivates him, how he learns best, the time of day he's most attentive, etc.) in a nearly one-on-one setting. Therefore, when a child is homeschooled, learning the same amount of information as in a traditional school should only take up to one-and-one half hours per day. That leaves most of the day free for the child. Just as important, learning happens in those "free" hours as well, and is even more valuable. This leads me to my second reason for homeschooling – play!

Reason 2: Play is Supremely Important

Imagination is more important than knowledge. Knowledge is limited. Imagination encircles the world. Albert Einstein

Decades of research has proven that play is the best way for our children to learn. Many studies have led to the following commonly accepted conclusions:[48]

- Children who are pushed into regimented academic instruction too early display less creativity and enthusiasm for learning than their peers.
- Children who memorize isolated facts early in life show less long-term retention than their peers.
- Children who learn through play develop social and emotional skills, which are critical for long term success, faster than their peers.
- Children starting first grade with a formal reading background were compared to other first graders without formal reading instruction who spent more time in play-based environments. The children who got the reading instruction performed better during the first grade but not by the end of the year. And, they were much more depressed than the other children.
- Stimulating play environments facilitate progress to higher levels of thought throughout childhood.

---

[48] Hirsh-Pasek, K., Ph.D. Golinkoff, R. M., Ph.D. (2003). *Einstein never used flashcards: How our children really learn and why they need to play more and memorize less.* Holtzbrinck Publishers

- Children who spend most of their time playing have more advanced language skills and literacy development than children who spend time with structured school activities.
- Play enhances problem solving, social skills, advanced cognitive skills and attention span.

Learning through play, pursing self-initiated interests, and following curiosities is the way infants learn and there is no reason to believe people will stop learning that way after a particular age. Therefore, left untouched, humans will pursue interests, explore, and learn in their environments.[49] Creativity and independent thinking are the result of intrinsic motivation that comes through child-centered play. Once play is taken away and replaced with school tasks, intrinsic motivation also disappears, and is replaced with extrinsic motivation. Schools are set up to force some children to learn before they are developmentally ready and before they are interested, which ensures the need for extrinsic rewards to entice the children to cooperate.

There is convincing evidence that children learn the best and the most through play and that forced learning does not pay off. Academic preschools, compared to play-based preschools, produce children who are less creative and more anxious. Play enhances problem solving, social skills and attention span, as well. Testing and academic goals can undermine creativity and lead children to become stressed, frightened and self-conscious.[50]

---

[49] Estroff-Marano, H. (1999, July/August). The power of play. *Psychology Today*

[50] Deci, E. L., Koestner, R., Ryan, R. M. (1999). A meta-analytic review of experiments examining the effects of extrinsic rewards on intrinsic motivation. *Psychological Bulletin, 125,* 627-668

Children's success later in school is directly correlated to the amount of time spent playing early in life. Children who attend formal preschools based on adult-led instruction show slower academic progress by forth grade than children who didn't attend preschool and spent the majority of time on self-directed activities including play. The culprit seems to be the introduction of formalized learning experiences too early for the child's developmental status.[51]

Play is vital to our health and play is the key to creativity and imagination. Creativity and imagination are the keys to happiness and success as individuals and as a human race.[52] Below are some famous quotes about play:

- "You can discover more about a person in an hour of play than in a year of conversation." – Plato
- "Play is the highest form of research." - Albert Einstein
- "We do not stop playing because we grow old. We grow old because we stop playing." - George Bernard Shaw
- "You've achieved success in your field when you don't know whether what you're doing is work or play." - Warren Beatty
- "If you want creative workers, give them enough time to play." -John Cleese

Homeschooling my daughter will allow her to play all day long. Therefore, she will be learning all day long (versus memorizing all day long, as she would do in school). Even the most formal methods of homeschooling only require roughly

[51] Elkind, D. (2003). *Miseducation: Preschoolers at risk*. New York: Random House.
[52] Henderson, S. (2002). The correlates of inventor motivation, creativity and achievement. *Stanford University*, 142 pages, AAT 3067866.

one-and-one half hours of formal instruction per day to keep pace with what is taught each day in traditional schools. That leaves the great majority of the day open for play, where the real learning takes place, where true growth occurs and where pure joy is experienced.

Reason 3: Retaining Intrinsic Motivation

I never teach my pupils; I only attempt to provide the conditions in which they can learn. Albert Einstein

Behavioral research has demonstrated that there are two kinds of motivation: extrinsic and intrinsic. Extrinsic motivation occurs when a person engages in a specific activity because of the reward expected. Intrinsic motivation develops when a person engages in a specific activity because it brings them internal satisfaction; an individual engages in the activity even if no one else is aware.[53]

With extrinsic motivation, the rewards can be removed at anytime, thereby eliminating any interest in continuing to perform the activity or task. Therefore, the control belongs to a force outside of the person.

Intrinsic motivation stays within a person. A person with intrinsic motivation will enjoy the task or activity regardless of outside control.[54] People with intrinsic motivation show more confidence, interest, and excitement about tasks. In addition, they show enhanced creativity, persistence, and performance. A 2002 study from Stanford University investigated the reasons why inventors invent. The study found most inventors to be largely

---

[53] Deci, E. L., Koestner, R., Ryan, R. M. (1999). A meta-analytic review of experiments examining the effects of extrinsic rewards on intrinsic motivation. *Psychological Bulletin, 125,* 627-668

[54] Deci, E. L. & Ryan, R. R. (2000). Self-determination theory and the facilitation of intrinsic motivation, social development, and well-being. *The American Psychologist, 55(1),* 68.

creative and intrinsically motivated. It was found that intrinsic motivation was strongly related to creativity and efficiency.[55]

Traditional schooling (such as public, private, Montessori) may be creating people (and a society) who are extrinsically motivated since traditional school is based upon extrinsic rewards. Extrinsic rewards are rewards that come from outside the individual. All traditional schools have extrinsic rewards as their foundation. Extrinsic rewards govern the way traditional schools operate. The high-level goal for traditional schooling is to move students up through each grade. Moving to the next grade is an extrinsic reward for achieving, behaving, and accomplishing in accordance to the school's defined expectations. In order to move to the next grade, the student must perform and behave in specific ways. In addition, the student must successfully complete smaller goals such as passing tests, completing homework assignments, and taking assessments. Grades received on these tests, assignments and assessments are extrinsic rewards for the desired performance. Receiving grades or evaluations on tests and assignments is common among all traditional schools, as is moving on to the next grade if performance is acceptable. Regardless of methods applied by individual teachers in individual schools, the overriding structure of traditional schools remains the same and is grounded in extrinsic rewards for desired performance and behavior.

Let's look at it this way. If there were no external motivators, including negative reinforcement, would students still sit quietly in their seats all day long and would they still strive to get certain grades on quizzes, and would they still spend hours memorizing? It's highly unlikely. External motivation is what drives students in traditional schools. If you take away the

---

[55] Henderlong, J. (2002). The effects of praise on children's intrinsic motivation. *Psychological Bulletin*, 128(5), 774-795.

external motivators, then most, if not all students would cease to perform and behave in ways the school system desires.

Prior to entering school, children show high levels of intrinsic motivation. There have been many studies showing that intrinsic motivation sharply declines once children enter school and the decline continues yearly with the largest drops at 3rd grade and 8th grade.[56]

Why is intrinsic motivation more desirable? Well, in addition to leading to creativity and innovation, people with intrinsic motivation show more confidence, self-esteem, and excitement about tasks and their lives in general.[57] Intrinsic motivation produces deeper engagement in learning, higher levels of performance, better conceptual learning, and higher persistence at learning activities.[58] If someone is engaging in a task mainly because of an external reward (or avoiding a negative reinforcement), then if that reward is taken away, the interest in the task goes away. With intrinsic motivation, it doesn't matter what other people think, say, or do. The motivation to do the task was never in their control in the first place.

I want my daughter to spend the majority of her time engaging in activities because she wants to engage in them, for her own reasons, her own enjoyment, her own fulfillment and her own desires to learn. I don't want her happiness and feelings of success to be tied to receiving external rewards. If that was the case, then someone else would always control her feelings and

---

[56] Kohn, A. (2003). Studies find reward often no motivator: Creativity and intrinsic interest diminish if task is done for gain.

[57] Kasser, T., & Ryan, R. M. (1996). Further examining the American dream: Differential correlates of intrinsic and extrinsic goals. *Personality and Social Psychology Bulletin, 22,* 280-287

[58] Vansteenkiste, M., Ryan, R.M. and Deci, E.L. (2008) 'Self-determination theory and the explanatory role of psychological needs in human well-being', in L. Bruni, F. Comim and M. Pugno (eds), Capabilities and Happiness, pp. 187-223. Oxford: Oxford University Press

her opinion of herself. I don't want her to be focused on comparing herself to others or doing something for the purpose of being judged, tested, or graded by others, especially when those "others" may not know her very well; they may not be people she should be looking up to or taking direction from. If she constantly does things for the purpose of satisfying other people rather than herself, then she gives up what is meaningful and important to her – and becomes an approval chaser.

I do not want her to spend the vast majority of her days engaged in tasks mainly for external rewards and the goals of others. If she does this, then when she becomes an adult, she'll have no idea what *she* enjoys, what *she's* naturally good at, what *she* wants to do/learn/say. It is my job to help her become an adult who can create her own happiness, independent of other's rewards, punishments and opinions. It is my job to help her become an adult who can find the inner motivation to search for new ideas on her own without being told what's important to know, learn, achieve.

There are many different methods of homeschooling, such as traditional, eclectic, and unschooling. Even the most stringent method requires no more than a couple hours of "formal" education per day. Even if external rewards for performance are used during that small amount of time, it's still far, far fewer hours per day than traditional schools. So, relatively speaking, a small amount of time may be spent doing things for external rewards, or for the satisfaction of others. If the unschooling method is used, then zero hours per day are spent doing anything that requires external motivation.

I know my child. I know her preferred learning styles, the time of day she's most open to learning, what types of learning activities blend best with her personality, and so on. Therefore, it's very easy for me to pepper in learning so that it becomes a natural part of her day, and something she actively pursues on her own without prompting from me. Unschooling allows me to impart learning without any external motivators at all. However, even if I was to use the most formal homeschooling method, which relies on a curriculum with tests and grades, it would still only take a maximum of a couple hours per day. Focusing on external rewards for such a small number of hours isn't likely to cause someone to build an entire lifestyle around pandering to external rewards.

Reason 4: Depth of Learning

The first half of my life I went to school, the second half of my life I got an education. *Mark Twain*

One of the things I remember most about school was the bells, along with the other indicators that it was time to move on to the next class. I remember many occasions where I was sitting in class and finally "getting it" with a subject and then a bell would ring and a teacher would nonchalantly tell us to pack up our things and move to the next class. Huh? Didn't she know that I had spent weeks trying to figure this stuff out? Now that I'm finally getting it and I'm knee-deep engaged in a task, is she *really* telling me it's time to stop? Didn't she know that this was a pivotal time for me, if I was ever going to figure this out, and become genuinely interested in it? Didn't she care?

The answer is - she didn't know and she didn't care. How could she? She barely knew me and had 30 other students to shuffle along. And, what if she did know and care? She had no control; the next class was coming into the classroom and I had to pack up and move along. I had to forget the topic at hand and move to the next.

What do bells in school teach us? When they ring it's time to stop what you are doing, put everything away, and move on to the next class, activity, or task. Whatever you are doing becomes unimportant when the bell rings. It doesn't matter how much you liked what you were doing; it doesn't matter how much you were learning; it doesn't matter that you just now had an "ah-ha" moment with the task; and it doesn't matter that you *wanted* to continue with the task. School bells teach us not to delve too deeply into anything because the bell will ring and we'll have to move on anyway. Even if we are interested, we don't become too engrossed because we know the bell is not far off. When this happens all day, everyday, we develop an inability to engage in a task long enough to become truly interested and passionate about it. We learn to just skim the surface of all topics; to do enough to get by but don't dare get too involved because it's not that important and if you get too interested, you'll be forced to give it up and move along anyway.

My goal for Genevieve is to allow her to follow her interests to the level and depth she desires. If she becomes thoroughly engrossed in astrology and spends days and nights looking through her telescope and reading astrology books then I don't want that interest minimized or halted. I want her to get as deeply involved as she wants and only when she's ready to move on, will she have to do so. It's important to me that she learns to follow her interests, glean everything she wants to out of a topic, and then make her own decision about when to move on to something else. It's of lesser importance to me, that she becomes adept at skimming the surface of multiple topics. It's of lesser importance to me that she learns to quickly cast aside an interest at the whim of someone else. I'm not at all interested in putting her into an environment where she's told that it's extremely important to learn X, Y, and Z, but only during this particular hour and only until someone else says "time's up".

By homeschooling Genevieve, I'm able to carefully watch her interests and allow her to delve as deeply into topics as she chooses. I am able to see when she's finally "getting it" and I can allow her all the time and space she needs to fully explore the subject. I send the message that her interests are important and she is free to spend as much time learning something as she wants. Because homeschooling takes so few hours per day, it leaves a lot of time for delving very deeply into topics. It also leaves a lot of time for exploring multiple topics to see what interests her.

Reason 5: Reliance on Being Led

I suppose it is because nearly all children go to school nowadays, and have things arranged for them, that they seem so forlornly unable to produce their own ideas. Agatha Christie

One of the most tragic phrases I hear children use regularly is "I'm bored". What does that really mean? Children say this when they believe that there is nothing to do, or when they can't *think* of anything to do. This phrase is sad for two reasons: 1) the child doesn't *believe* she can create her own enjoyment or entertainment, and 2) the child expects to "do" rather than to "be".

How does a child come to believe that she cannot create her own enjoyment? When children are between the ages of one and three, they are busy, busy, busy. They explore, observe, investigate and create. A good deal of their time is unstructured and they find ways to fill it. Everything fascinates them, so there is generally not a great need for structured activities or continually finding them things to do. There is no reason for that to change as children grow. Sure, as they get older, they become more familiar with their environments so the things that used to hold their attention no longer will. But, as they grow, they can comprehend more, which enables them to view things differently; everything old is new again as the brain develops. The world doesn't become less captivating as you get older – the opposite happens.

So, why do children go from being able to make up their own games and spend hours creating enjoyment out of "nothing", to saying "I'm bored" every ten minutes unless they've been given a structured activity or task to do? Because, at some point, children become accustomed to being *led*. One culprit that leads to perceived boredom is too much passive entertainment. Children who watch a lot of TV and movies get used to being passive observers rather than active participants. They don't create their own ideas and actively follow them through to see what happens next and learn from their experience. Instead, they are presented with ideas that were someone else's and led down a pre-determined path.

While passive entertainment plays a role in the declining ability of children to create their own ideas and entertainment, the major offender is traditional schooling. Until children go to school, their days are mostly unstructured. Children have blocks of hours to fill and must use their imaginations to generate ideas to fill that time. They learn to trust their own ability to create enjoyment for themselves, which greatly helps self-esteem. When children go to school, most of their days are spent doing what someone else tells them to do. This isn't all bad. In the early years of schooling (pre-kindergarten – first grade), most of what that "someone" is telling them to do is enjoyable for the child and in alignment with their current interests and level of brain development.

Nonetheless, the child starts to become conditioned to follow what someone else is telling them to do. They start to believe and trust that someone else knows what they should do, what they should learn, and what they should know. They start to believe that whatever they (the child) want to do, learn, and know is *not* important.

It's not the content that is objectionable in the early school years. It's the life lesson that is so unfortunate: The child learns that her ideas and interests are of little value. Instead, the teacher's ideas are more relevant, more important. The child learns to please the teacher rather than herself. She becomes less significant in her own eyes, as she propels other's ideas into the center of importance. She starts to mistrust her feelings about what is important and learns to put her desires and interests aside.

Once a child enters the third grade, things get worse. Until this point, the life lesson described above is heartbreaking but at least much of the content presented is somewhat interesting to the child. Around the third grade the content starts to deviate from the child's interest. This is why intrinsic motivation drops drastically at about third grade (and takes a second dip around eighth grade). Many children give up much of *themselves*. They have already become painfully aware that what they are interested in is of little importance, but that was somewhat okay when what was being taught was fairly interesting. By the third grade, they now know their desires don't count, and they are subjected to content and subjects that don't hold their attention and is out of alignment with their brain development. Children know they don't have a choice; they must allow themselves to be force-fed content and try to get through it. They push their interests and desires to the back of their minds and become followers, with nearly every hour of their day directed by an adult.

For much of the day, it's the teacher who is orchestrating the child's time. With school comes homework and after school activities, where coaches are directing, and parents are pushing for homework completion. Children learn to sit back and let someone else tell them what to do, and how and when to do it. They rarely get the opportunity to come up with their own ideas and be creative. Oh sure, an occasional assignment requires some creativity but contrast that to life *before* school when children were creative for most of the day, every day. Children unlearn *the* most important element of life which is how to create. All of life is about creation and everything revolves around idea generation which *requires* strong creative ability and strong intrinsic motivation.

When children are home from school for summer break, they frequently say "I'm bored". Parents find it annoying and often give their kids some ideas to keep them from hanging around and nagging them about being bored. However, this is so much more than just annoying; it's a sign that the child is no longer generating her own ideas. She probably *can* but she is so used to being led, directed, told and entertained, that she's grown to expect it. Idea generation takes work in the form of creative thinking, which isn't something encouraged during school days. If children were truly encouraged to think outside of the box and stretch their imaginations during school, mass chaos would ensue; children would be coming up with new games to play, ideas about what to learn and how to learn it, and challenging teacher's ideas for lessons.

Another reason that hearing "I'm bored" should be alarming is because the child is looking for something to do and "being" isn't even considered. We are not human doings but human beings. However, when a child's day is filled up by someone else and the focus is on doing, the child forgets how to just "be". The child is restless unless she is doing and is no longer comfortable just *being* with herself. One of the reasons children aren't comfortable being with themselves revolves around their perceived loss of control when adults begin force feeding them content all day long and disregarding the child's interests and desires. When the child realizes that how they want to spend their time is completely irrelevant – something that was previously very important - much of their intrinsic motivation is traded in for extrinsic motivation. Being *with* their selves becomes less comfortable as they detach from themselves, which they must do to cope with their new reality that revolves around satisfying others.

We are thrilled to watch young children create their own fun and make up games and decide how to spend their time. We are amazed at what they come up with and how fast they learn when they are truly interested in something and pursuing it of their own accord. What children want to learn is important; the way they want to learn it is important; and when they want to learn it is important. If we let children direct their own learning, they will remember it, use it, and build on it. If we try to direct their learning toward what *we* think is important, chances are they will not *learn* it but instead, *memorize* it, and *forget* it. But, the worst thing that happens is that the child loses his interest in learning anything.

So, for at least twelve years, children have lifestyles whereby they are followers, being led on an hour-by-hour basis by someone else – possibly by someone they don't know well, trust, or respect. They are being told what to do, when to do it, and how to do it - day in and day out. What *aren't* they doing while all of this is going on? They aren't thinking for themselves. They aren't learning to trust their own opinions about what's valuable to them. They aren't gaining confidence and self-esteem by selecting their own goals based on their intrinsic desires, developing plans for achieving them, and accomplishing them. Instead, they are learning to doubt their thoughts, intuition and feelings, discarding them in favor of the "right" ones dictated by an adult who is not likely their parent. They learn not to question anything because they believe they are powerless, which they are, because they are children. Only the adults in their lives can change this reality for them, unfortunately.

This reliance on being led, and learning not to question authority, while going along with the majority, haunts just about everyone throughout their lives. We are forever in a classroom with someone else teaching and leading, while the majority group plays the role of the classmates. Adults mistrust their own beliefs, ideas and opinions. After all, these didn't count or matter for at least twelve years of their lives. You watch what the "class" is doing in all aspects of your life and if what they are doing is what the "teacher" is advocating, then in most cases, you follow along. How could you not? And so we push our needs, desires, and questions aside, believing everyone else must know best, especially if there is a "teacher" guiding us. We quietly sit in our seats in the "school room of life" and push what's important to us aside while waiting for the "next class".

Think about this: What if you never learned that what you want doesn't count? What if you never learned that a teacher always knows more than you do? What if you never learned that if ninety-nine percent of people are doing X, Y, and Z, it's probably better than what you were going to do? Instead, what if you lived a life where what you wanted to do was of utmost importance, and your opinions, thoughts, desires were as valid as anyone else's regardless of age or stature? Even if everyone else was doing something, it was perfectly acceptable for you to do/think/feel something completely different and you would be positively recognized for your individuality. How drastically different would your life be now?

Reason 6: Integrated Subjects

The child is curious. He wants to make sense out of things, find out how things work, gain competence and control over himself and his environment. He does not merely observe the world around him, he does not shut himself off from the strange, complicated world around him, but tastes it, touches it, hefts it, bends it, breaks it ... School is not a place that gives much time, or opportunity, or reward, for this kind of thinking and learning. John Holt

Art was my favorite class and I found History to be very boring. I was great at English but I was horrible at Math. Subjects in grade school are divided into isolated topic areas. Children in school go from one isolated subject to the next. They form opinions about subjects early on and those opinions have a lifelong impact. I never liked math in school because I wasn't good at it. Or, was I bad at math because I didn't like it? Who knows which came first?

As I was preparing to enter college, I found myself very interested in Accounting. But Accounting was mostly math so I almost poo-poo'd it. I recalled the words of many grade school teachers: "Julie excels in so many areas but she'll never be good at math." Regardless, I enrolled in some Accounting classes and they contained a lot of math, which was difficult for me. But, while they were mostly math, the context was intriguing. The math was wrapped up in appealing context that ranged from making smart business decisions to maximizing tax benefits. So, the math wasn't really math; it became a tool to use in order to excel in many areas of life and business. The teachers never taught math as if it was an isolated skill to master or a means to an end. They never taught it within the context of short story problems that involved two trains or varying pieces of rope. What they taught was how to make good business decisions, with an "oh-by-the-way, here are some tools to help you do it" teaching style, most of which involved math.

Before children enter school, they learn a little bit about all topics in a holistic way. They relate the new material they are learning to something they already know and it's all anchored by context and meaning. For example, when a child sets the table for dinner, the goal is to have dinner and setting the table is just a step towards that goal. The child learns that there are four people in the family so they need four plates and four forks and four napkins. If they pull out three forks, they learn that pulling out one more will equal four. It's not "math" to them; they are setting the table for dinner, learning, and having fun. Because the activity has context and meaning, they are more apt to remember the math that helped them obtain their goal. Had the child been taught how to add, in an isolated way, it would have taken much longer for it to "stick" and recalling it would be more difficult.

Children are whole people. When we look at them we don't look intensely at one arm, and then at one foot, and then at the neck and consider each part separately. When we look out at the ocean we don't focus first on the smell, and then move on to the feel of the air, and then move on to the color of the water. We take it all in as a whole with all parts interacting and relating to each other in a way that creates the entire, memorable scene.

Success as a student, and as a person, always depends on how you pull it all together as a whole. It's never made up of individual parts. Let's take tennis as an example. Let's say we have a tennis pro and an amateur tennis player. The tennis pro is well-known and at the top of her game. The amateur is taking lessons. Now, that amateur can be taught to have a perfect forehand and a perfect backhand and a perfect serve. In fact, on a

101

skill-by-skill basis, many amateurs have been proven to have much better skills than the pros, when you isolate individual skills. If an amateur were to execute each isolated skill just as well as a pro, would you expect them to *be* as good as a pro? Of course not.

In like manner, many people have individual skills at, or above, the level of pros. That is almost entirely meaningless. The only thing that matters is the whole – how it's all put together. Pros can have weaker skills in every skill area of a game but still win over and over against an amateur. It's all about how those skills are pulled together to make the whole.

When children are young, they learn in a holistic way, and they retain what they've learned. Once they learn to walk, they don't seem to forget it. Once they learn basic math from tasks like setting the table, sending out party invitations (counting out the number of invitations, stamps, etc.) they never seem to forget it. Once they learn basic colors from identifying them on the clothes they wear and household objects, they don't forget them. Once they learn to read basic words because they need that skill to read signs, etc. they don't forget it. They don't forget these things because they are learning in order to get to a goal and the learning has meaning and is surrounded by context. Learning is *not* the goal. There is a purpose to what they learn, a meaning and a context. The learning is *related* to some goal they hope to achieve or some piece of knowledge they already have that is important to them. As soon as learning becomes *the* goal without meaningful purpose and context, children tune out. They start forgetting and they begin to dread classes, and they lose interest – possibly forever.

When children learn in a holistic way, they are developing their emotional, social, creative, spiritual, and intellectual potentials. They are investing in themselves completely and totally. Contrast this to learning one subject at a time where the goal *is* learning the subject; there is no specific reason, no context, no meaning, and nothing to tie the learning to the child's "self". In order for children to learn in a holistic way, we must know what is important to them, what they already know, and what *their* near-term goals are as children. We need to capitalize on what can be learned by helping them achieve those near-term goals, while relating the learning to something they already know, and relating it to something that is important to them.

Learning is all about relationships and connections. Relationships and connections are not at all in sync with isolated school subjects. Isolating subjects is about rejecting relationships and denying connections. Learning that is grounded in context, meaning, and purpose, will come about easily and naturally and last a lifetime. However, the learning program must be highly individualized.

Homeschooling, using the unschooling method, will allow me to teach Genevieve a holistic way whereby subjects are not taught in an isolated way. Only I know what my daughter already knows, what's important to her, her short-term goals, and how to provide optimum context and meaning, as well as relating and connecting learning to her goals and previous knowledge. There is no way that someone other than a family member would know her to this degree. By homeschooling, I am able to carefully monitor what is being learned as well as being able to see the subtle changes in her goals and what she values, and continuously cater to her interests and needs with new learning nuggets that will fit in seamlessly and "stick" with her. I can ensure that no one subject is ever isolated so memorization will rarely be needed. I can ensure that she's learning new skills, knowledge, and behaviors in a way that utilizes her intellect and connects with her social, creative, emotional, and spiritual aspects.

Reason 7: What's Going on Outside of School

I believe that school makes complete fools of our young men,
because they see and hear nothing of ordinary life there.
Petronius *(Satyricon)*

As adults we are fully aware of the value of time. We carefully weigh our options and look at the pros and cons of selecting one activity over another. When we choose to engage in a particular activity at the expense of another, we look at the opportunity lost by not engaging in the other activity. We may choose to play golf, or stay late at work, rather than attend our child's tee-ball game. When making that choice we carefully think about what we are missing by not attending the game. Anytime we choose not to engage, we think about what we are missing. A good majority of our days are spent considering our options with regard to how to spend our time. And it should be. How we spend our time is extremely important; we don't have much of it and we can't waste it.

Is a child's time any less valuable than an adult's? It's actually *more* valuable. We only think it's less valuable because children are young and we envision them as having an endless supply of time. The way children spend their time is what defines their lives and shapes who they will become as adults. Once they become adults, how they spend their time doesn't have nearly as profound an impact.

When I look back at my childhood, do I think it was a good use of my time to be in school for six to seven hours a day, and then do one to three hours of homework each day for twelve years? Let me see…I was one of the lucky kids. I was popular, played team sports, and got good grades. I can't recall any glaringly negative experiences - no bullying, no feeling left-out, no struggles to get good grades. Was it a good use of my time? No, but not because of what I spent my time doing while in school. Rather, because of what I *missed* while in school.

Let's be honest about one thing: We all know that to comprehend everything we learned in school, even the useless material, did not need to take us six to seven hours per day, plus homework time. It could have all been learned in much less than a quarter of that time, if it was taught outside of a school environment, and if it was taught when interest and cognitive ability were in alignment. Currently, homeschool families are guided toward spending no more than one to two hours per day on teaching/learning activities, if their goal is to stay in step with local school districts.

True learning primarily occurs while navigating through interactions with new people, new environments, new situations, and new feelings. Real life involves these things on a daily basis. School is staged. It's a practice area for life rather than a place to live life. The stage of school is very unrealistic. The kids in the classroom are all the same age, and they all follow one set of rules that an adult dictates to them. The environment remains mostly the same everyday, and there are few unique situations that require unique solutions. The material is carefully crafted and fed to the children. Furthermore, much of what is "taught" in school is actually not being learned; it's being memorized. It's no great feat to memorize thousands of facts, or learn to do any task that can be broken down into a repeatable process. These things only have value if you can place them within context, give them meaning, or use them in the "big picture".

Living life provides context and meaning. Life is the big picture. By homeschooling Genevieve, I can teach her everything she needs to know in about an hour each day and then spend the rest of the day providing context and meaning and tying it all into the big picture. By actually living life, she encounters new and unique environments, people of different ages, situations that elicit unfamiliar feelings. There is no substitute for actually living and actually experiencing. It can't be staged.

The most important thing for a child to learn is how to be creative. All of life is based on creation. Being creative requires a solid relationship with self, and draws upon the true nature of the soul. Creativity requires a good imagination and intrinsic motivation. If a child has a good imagination and is creative, everything else will follow – all other intellectual knowledge will come as the child seeks it out.

So, what does a child miss while spending all of those hours in school and with homework? Family time. More than three decades of research shows that families have greater influence over a child's success in life than any other factor, including schools. Children learn the most, not from people who teach them, but from people who talk *with* them. In families, people talk *with* each other. When children are homeschooled, they get to be with family members for the majority of their day. Family members, who care about them, talk with them, understand them, and empathize with them.

What else does a child miss out on? Time to live; time that could be spent interacting with people of all ages within the context of normal life; time that could be spent outside, interacting with nature; time that could be spent encountering an endless stream of unique situations and experiences; time that could be spent developing a superb imagination; time that could be spent letting intrinsic motivation guide her tasks and activities; time that could be spent creating. Imagination and creativity are a person's main tools for creating their reality, and ultimately determine their success.

By homeschooling Genevieve, I am able to teach her everything she needs to know in a fraction of the time it would take in a school setting, leaving the majority of our days free for the most important things in life.

Reason 8: Healthy Lifestyle

I have never let my schooling interfere with my education.
Mark Twain

You're already aware that I'm not allowing Genevieve to watch TV and one of the primary reasons is the negative impact that TV has on the health of children and adults. When I was in school, being pudgy was considered cute because it was unique – most kids were fit and trim back then. Those days are long, long gone. Now, most kids are pudgy and many are well beyond pudgy. It's not cute. It's not just unhealthy, it's downright dangerous because it shortens lives and lessens the quality of life.

My goal as a parent is to make decisions that will ensure my daughter will be as happy and healthy as possible throughout her life. I can't possibly meet that goal while allowing her to watch TV at the same time. Many studies show that the odds are stacked against me with regard to the negative impact of TV on health. Traditional schools are unhealthy as well. Most have soda pop machines and vending machines that provide chips, candy and other junk. School cafeterias also peddle unhealthy food. Many schools have TVs in them that frequently advertise junk food.

All of this makes it nearly impossible for the parent's message about health to get through to the child. The child thinks to herself, *Mom's saying junk food is bad for me but then how come when I get to school everyone's eating it and there are vending machines and the school cafeteria sells it – so how bad can it be? Mom must be wrong.* It becomes harder for mom's message to be the most influential message; it falls into the background and mom gets tired of the battle and grudgingly gives in. Anyone who still says, "Come-on, there's nothing wrong with a little junk food" is in denial about the state of this nation's obesity crisis and the myriad of health issues that go along with it. Facing reality requires us to make difficult decisions and sometimes it's just easier to be in denial because it gives us permission to disregard our responsibility.

Homeschooling Genevieve allows me to be her main influencer with regard to healthy lifestyle choices. I can incorporate exercise throughout the day and emphasize the importance of it. I can lead by example and let her see me living a healthy lifestyle, and I can talk about how good it makes me feel and how good it is for my body and mind. She can see me eating healthy food for each meal and learn from that. I can prepare all of her meals and know exactly what she's getting. She can get a good solid foundation from me, and chances are, that will stay with her throughout her life.

Reason 9: Real-World Socialization

The difference between school and life? In school you're taught a lesson and then given a test. In life, you're given a test that teaches you a lesson. Tom Bodett

I can hear some people say, "But, but, but……what about socialization?" Many people will tell me that they wholeheartedly agree with all of my homeschooling reasons, and they even add a handful of reasons of their own. However, when I ask why they don't homeschool, they bring up socialization. This is not truly a reason people don't homeschool. This is something they *point* to as a reason. And, they do it for many reasons. Some people use it as a scapegoat when they know the real reason they don't homeschool is because they like having the kids out of the house all day. Some people hold it up as a reason because they don't want to have to admit to themselves that they send their kids to school because everyone else is doing it and they don't trust themselves to make a decision that goes against the majority. After all, they went to school too, and are conditioned to follow the majority without question.

The truth is, homeschooling allows children to be socialized in the real world. They interact with people of different ages and in different environments on a daily basis. They interact with animals and nature. Nearly every community has an abundance of homeschool clubs and classes. Local libraries offer homeschool only reading groups, art studios offer homeschool only classes, skating rinks offer homeschool only skate times, dance studios offer homeschool only classes. Most communities have multiple homeschool sports leagues, homeschool proms, homeschool Girl Scout troupes, and homeschool 4-H clubs. If that's not enough, nearly every community has multiple homeschool co-ops which offer every class imaginable for every skill level desired.

In the real world, people aren't grouped by age and the leaders aren't always older than the "followers". Rarely, do I find myself in a grocery store where everyone else is forty-two years old. When I go to work, my co-workers aren't all forty-two with the bosses being older than the subordinates. The instructor of my Yoga class isn't older than I am but yet, I'm following her directions. Most of my friends are in their early 30s, some are in their 20s, a few are in their 40s and 50s. In the real world, people must learn to interact with people of every age, and talk appropriately to the very young and the very old. They must understand different ages and the complexities that accompany them.

Homeschooling allows children to interact in the real world all day long, encountering people of every age and learning that younger people can be more knowledgeable and be leaders. They learn that older people don't necessarily know more and shouldn't be listened to and followed blindly. The socialization children get by living in the real world, without the artificial school setting, helps prepare them for the real world and gives them the skills to interact with all kinds of people on all kinds of levels, without having to categorize and group according to age.

Reason 10: Lifestyle

Thank goodness I was never sent to school; it would have rubbed off some of my originality. Beatrix Potter.

Homeschooling allows us to have a more relaxed and natural lifestyle. For example, Genevieve gets to wake up whenever she feels like it. I can't recall one single time whereby we've had to wake her up for anything. She wakes up naturally ever morning and there's no reason for that to change. She gets as much sleep as she needs every night. Sometimes she wakes up at 7:00 and then falls back asleep for an hour. Sometimes she wakes up at 7:00 and gets right up. Sometimes she wakes up at 8:30. It really doesn't matter; wake-up time is dictated by the amount of sleep her body needs.

We schedule our family vacations whenever we want without having to consider what might be going on at school. And, we schedule them when the schools are still in session so we can avoid crowds and lines. We go to parks, skating rinks, ceramic studios, planetariums, museums, theatres in the middle of the day and have the places virtually to ourselves.

We work learning into our lifestyle so there's no "stopping" life to make time for learning and then resuming life when learning has occurred. Living life is learning – it's all intertwined.

Summary

They say that we are better educated than our parent's generation. What they mean is that we go to school longer. It is not the same thing. *Richard Yates*

As anyone who has studied history is aware, the American education system began with the primary purpose of creating loyal workers who would be trained to follow orders. This was a way to ensure that those in power remained in power, and that they had enough laborers and followers to work in their businesses and keep them profitable. Those in power did not want independent or creative thinking that would challenge their reign. In order to ensure that happened, the system had to separate children from their parents at an early age so that they could be given orders and be influenced without parental intervention or contradiction. In addition, separating children from their families at young ages essentially took away their security and support system which is necessary to create subservient and "follower" behavior. Creating this type of school system was a deliberate act with roots in 19th century industrialism.

However, just because this is how the American education system began does not mean that this is the purpose today. Let's assume that the purpose of today's schools is to create highly intelligent, unique, imaginative and creative people who will invent, discover and create. Do you think the output of today's school system more clearly matches the original purpose of schools, or my assumed purpose? Are schools creating a society of people who are trained to follow orders without question, learn what they are told without being given reasons why, and behave in ways that will elicit external rewards from the school system? Of course they are. Regardless of the purpose

113

of today's school system, the outcome is in absolute alignment with the historical roots of the American education system.

Has our country benefited from having the vast majority of the population become worker-bee followers who don't challenge orders or question those in power? Well, yes, we have benefited as a country, but not as individuals. However, our country won't benefit from this mentality going forward. Throughout the agricultural age, industrial age, and information age, we've depended on a vast employee base comprised of employees who would listen to orders, follow instructions, and be enticed by extrinsic rewards. These time periods needed very few leaders and a whole lot of followers. As we are all painfully aware by now, most of the "follower" jobs can easily be sent "offshore". Any job that can be broken down into a set of steps or processes can be taught to anyone in the world and performed much more cheaply than by American labor.

We are now entering the conceptual age, which will be made up of creators, inventors, idea generators, out-of-the-box thinkers and risk takers. In the conceptual age, the success of America will depend on our ability to create independent thinkers who challenge the status quo, challenge those in power and challenge traditionally accepted ideas. These will be highly imaginative and creative people; the kind of people who will be intrinsically motivated. Our current school system is not even remotely set up to facilitate this kind of output. If we want our children to succeed in the upcoming conceptual age, there is no question that sending them to traditional schools will hinder their success.

Schools cannot teach individuals; they can only teach groups. Any abnormalities must be normalized so that the group is teachable. For example, Dyslexia has been labeled a disability by traditional school systems. Children with Dyslexia have difficulty being taught with the rest of the class. With Dyslexia there is a lack of linear thinking which makes reading and writing a bit more difficult to learn, if it's being taught in a linear way. But is it really a disability? Studies have shown that self-made millionaires are *4 times* more likely to be Dyslexic than the general public. The non-linear thinking pattern inherent in Dyslexia is highly desirable by businesses. Employers hiring for upper level management positions administer assessments designed to find people with non-linear thinking patterns. This is because non-linear thinking allows people to see the big picture. Charles Schwab has said that the secret to his success is his Dyslexia. Richard Branson, who has shaken up the retail music and airline industries, also credits his Dyslexia for his success. Homeschooling can teach the *whole* individual and "disabilities" like Dyslexia are no longer disabilities. This unique way of thinking may require a different approach to facilitate reading and writing, but so what? The benefits of it far outweigh the negatives.

According to the Department of Education, there are roughly 1.8-2.5 million homeschooled children in America. This number has doubled in the past decade and is expected to triple or quadruple in the next decade. Homeschooling is growing by 7 percent to 12 percent per year. There is substantial research asserting the success of homeschooling. Each year, the results are very similar. Homeschooled students score nearly double the national average in the areas of reading, language, science, social studies and math, for all age levels. Colleges, including Ivy League colleges are clamoring to admit homeschooled students and most have special admission processes for homeschooled students to make it easier for them to apply. This is because, not only do they show impressive academic success, they also have a broad diversity of interests and experiences that colleges feel will enhance the educational experiences of the campus population.

While it is true that homeschool parents as a whole have higher income levels and more advanced degrees than U.S.

averages, this does not have an impact on homeschool test scores. The test scores of homeschooled children living close to the poverty level were not much different than the scores of children from wealthy homes. They all scored nearly double what their non-homeschooled counterparts scored. Gender doesn't make a difference either. In homes where neither parent holds a college degree, the scores are in the same range – nearly double traditionally schooled children. However, in homes where both parents have a college degree, scores are a few points higher.

While all of this information is certainly interesting and may be important to some homeschooling parents, it isn't to me. You'll notice that none of my top ten reasons have anything to do with academic achievement or test scores. None of my reasons have anything to do with the content of what is taught, politics or religion. In my homeschool, the focus is on cultivating imagination and creativity and ensuring intrinsic motivation is left intact. With a good imagination and lots of creativity, everything else will follow. A person will learn what they need to learn in order to feed a strong imagination and a creative soul.

Now, let's look at homeschooling from a financial perspective. If homeschooling allows children to maintain their intrinsic motivation, spend more time with their families, spend more time playing and enjoying life, spend more time engaged in real-world social interactions, and have nearly double the academic success of traditionally schooled children, then why isn't homeschool heavily encouraged in public forums? Why don't we see advertisements on TV about the benefits of homeschooling and why aren't we seeing government endorsement of homeschooling?

Of course, you know the answer. Let's all say it together: *Nobody makes any money from homeschooling.* In fact, many people, businesses, and organizations will lose a lot of money if more people choose to homeschool. Traditional schooling is big, big business.

Homeschooling is completely and totally free. Sure, there are companies that sell homeschool curriculums, but they are not required and certainly not necessary. Nobody makes a dime if you decide to homeschool your child. There is no reason for anyone to promote it, advertise it, or endorse it, unless they truly believe in it and care about the education, well-being, and souls of human beings. And, as more people choose to homeschool, businesses, organizations and governments will lose more and more money. Thus, instead of seeing endorsements and advertising for homeschooling, you'll see the opposite. Already, there is increasing panic around the rise of homeschooling because of the money being lost by school systems and governments.

The fact is, homeschooling works. If it didn't work, nobody would be panicking about the rise in popularity. But, they are. If homeschooling led to children who were undereducated and maladjusted, nobody would object to it because money could be made from that. Businesses and governments would be able to profit from "helping" these undereducated, maladjusted children. But because homeschooling is so effective and is free, it's increasingly seen as a threat.

***The important thing is not to stop questioning.** Albert Einstein*

Afterword

We've covered a wide variety of topics together. I hope that what you've read has been thought provoking and has left you with more questions than answers. And, I hope that you will delve into those questions and rely on research, knowledge, experience, intuition and feelings in seeking answers. If your research, knowledge and experience point in one direction while your intuition and feelings point in another, than keep digging. You'll know you've arrived at the right answer when what's in your brain matches what's in your heart and soul.

The goals I set for myself as a parent, and my goals for my child, led me to decisions that are well outside the mainstream. Every parent has their own set of goals, and different goals will lead to different decisions. Being a parent is the most important job there is – by far. Every decision will have far reaching implications, as we all know. This can become overwhelming. We're afraid to make the wrong decision and the amount of information available about anything and everything is staggering. Many times we just give up and do what everyone else is doing.

Unvaccinated, Homeschooled, and TV-Free

Amazingly, people are more apt to "go with the flow" when there is more at stake. When the stakes are highest, it seems to make sense that people would spend the most time researching and questioning to come up with their own personal decisions. But, the opposite holds true. When the stakes are high, people spend the least amount of time researching and questioning, and they are more apt to do what everyone else is doing. We become paralyzed with fear of making the wrong decision. After all, if we do what everyone else is doing, we can't really be blamed if something goes wrong. We don't trust ourselves when it comes to the really important decisions. And, when we do begin researching and questioning and find that what we are coming up with isn't what everyone else is doing, we are likely to doubt ourselves and just give up and give in.

Once you've made an unconventional decision, the hardest part isn't behind you. After months of searching and questioning and sleepless nights and stress, you'll breathe a sigh of relief upon finally arriving at your decision. But, then you'll find yourself in uncomfortable situations whereby friends and family will question you, and you may feel compelled to explain your reasons and defend your decisions.

However, there is no need to explain or defend anything. If you try to explain your unconventional decisions, most people will automatically think you are judging them for making a different decision. In social situations, when you are being questioned, there is no way you could adequately explain a decision that likely took you months and months to arrive at.

In fact, someone who asks "why do you homeschool" actually thinks that you can give an answer in a couple of sentences. This is because their decision to send their child to school didn't likely require any thought on their part at all; they just did it because everyone else is doing it. Similarly, someone who asks what you have against vaccinations, likely vaccinated their child with no thought at all and truly believes you can give a quick explanation for your opposite choice.

The vast majority of these people never researched anything. They just did what everyone else was doing. So, when I hear someone say "ninety percent of people vaccinate, and they can't all be wrong", I know they don't understand what they are saying. Of that ninety percent, it's unlikely that more than five percent actually did the level of research that is done by the people who make unconventional decisions. I never care that people arrive at the same conclusions that I did. I only care that they personally put in a level of effort that corresponds to the importance of the decision. Most don't.

When I'm in a social situation and these kinds of questions are asked, I give general answers and just move on. You'll be able to tell the difference between people who actually want to know the answer and have an open mind, and those who ask because they are feeling judged by you and hope that something in your answer will validate their own, opposite decision.

After you've made your decision, there may be times when your resolve is challenged and it may seem easier to give in and go along. Shortly after my daughter turned one, she had a terrible accident that necessitated an ambulance ride to the hospital. I was out of my mind with grief. After spending several traumatic hours in the hospital with her, no fewer than five doctors tried to convince me to give her some vaccinations. The vaccines had nothing to do with the accident in any way. They just saw in her records that she wasn't vaccinated. One by one they took me aside and spent half an hour with me trying to convince me.

Unvaccinated, Homeschooled, and TV-Free

How did they try to convince me? Not with facts, studies, and statistics proving she'd be much healthier if she received vaccines, because those don't exist. Not with facts, studies, and statistics proving she'd be in danger if she didn't receive vaccines because those don't exist either. They talked mainly about the percentage of people who are vaccinated versus those who are unvaccinated. Their main argument was, "Everyone else is doing it and all those people can't be wrong. You're a well educated, smart lady so we know you'll do the right thing." Needless to say, this only helped convince me not to budge on the issue. On a follow-up visit about a week after we left the hospital, one of our doctors said "good for you" after it became clear that my daughter was not vaccinated.

Before I made any unconventional decisions, I rarely met people who had. Or so I thought. But, once you walk down this path, you'll begin to discover all kinds of people, in unlikely positions, who took a similar path. They just don't advertise it. You'll encounter doctors and nurses who share with you that they didn't vaccinate their children either. And, you'll meet scientists, psychologists and business executives, who homeschool their children. Many people, upon learning of your decisions, will feel empowered by the possibilities and choices available to them; they never thought of these things before and may not have known they had a choice. Many people, upon learning of your decisions, will feel threatened for whatever reason.

Ultimately, I've made the best decisions I can, questioning absolutely everything, researching all possibilities, and using all available data. And, I checked it all against my instincts and intuition. No expert or official will ever have the interest in my child to delve into every possibility and intimately analyze the impact of each option on my daughter. They don't have the interest, or the time, or the motivation to do such a thing. Only I do, and so, I did.

About the Author

Julie Cook owns a successful life coaching business (www.noregretslifecoaching.com), where she specializes in work/life balance, goal setting strategies, performance improvement at work, and parenting. She also works as a manager for a global technology company. Her most important job, however, is being a mom to her daughter, Genevieve.

Unvaccinated, Homeschooled and TV-Free: It's Not Just for Fanatics and Zealots is the culmination of five years of research. The original intent of the research was to provide Genevieve with information to help her understand why she is being raised differently than most children she will encounter.

Julie is currently working on several projects including a sequel to this book which will address her family's other unconventional decisions, an unschooling book, as well as a series of children's books specifically directed toward homeschooled children.

Julie lives with her daughter in Howell, MI.

References

Akin-Little, K. A. (2004). Extrinsic reinforcement in the classroom: Bribery or best practice. *School Psychology Review, 33(3),* 344-62.

Anderson, P.M., Butcher, K. F. (2006). *Childhood obesity: Trends and potential causes.* Dartmouth College.

Anderson-Levitt, K. (March, 2004). The schoolyard gate: Schooling and childhood in global perspective. *Childhood and Globalization.* Retrieved July 3, 2006, from http://www.newglobalhistory.org/docs/The%20schoolyard%20gate.pdf

Anju, M., Clayton, H., Sankar, C.S. (2008). Impact of multi-media case studies on improving intrinsic learning motivation of students. *Journal of Educational Technology Systems, 36(1),* 79-103.

Baker, Jeffrey (2002). *The pertussis controversy in Great Britain, 1974-1986.* Center for the Study of Medical Ethics and Humanities. Duke University.

Blumenfeld, S. L. (1999). The history of Public Education. *Practical Homeschooling Magazine, 30.*
Brock, B. (2007). *Living outside the box: TV-free families share their secrets.* Washington: Eastern Washington University Press.

British Columbia Centre for Disease Control and Laval University (2009). *Seasonal Flu Shot Linked to H1N1.*

Cave, S. M.D. (2001). *What your doctor may not tell you about children's vaccinations.* New York: Warner Books.

Coleman, Vernon M.D. Diptheria. Vernon Colman Health Letter. http://www.vernoncoleman.com/vaccines.htm

Coulter, Harris Ph.D. (1997). Childhood vaccinations and juvenile-onset (type 1) diabetes. http://www.whale.to/v/coulter.html

Crain, W. (2003). *Reclaiming childhood: Letting children be children in our achievement oriented society.* New York: Owl Books.

Creighton, C., M.D. (2009). *The vaccination myth: Courageous M.D. exposes the vaccination fraud.* CA: Createspace.

De Marsh, Q.B, (1941). The Effect of Depriving the Infant of its Placental Blood. *Journal of American Medical Association,* 116(23), 2568-2573.

De Melker, H.E., Schellekens, J.F., Neppelenbroek, S.E., Mooi, F.R., Rumke, H.C., Conyn-van Spaendonck, M.A. (2000). *Reemergence of pertussis in the highly vaccinated population of the Netherlands: observations on surveillance data.* Department of Infectious Disease Epidemiology, National Institute of Public Health and the Environment. Bilthoven, the Netherlands.

References

Deci, E. L. (1971). Effects of externally mediated rewards on intrinsic motivation. *Journal of Personality and Social Psychology, 18*, 105-115.

Deci, E. L., Koestner, R., Ryan, R. M. (1999). A meta-analytic review of experiments examining the effects of extrinsic rewards on intrinsic motivation. *Psychological Bulletin, 125*, 627-668.

Deci, E. L. & Ryan, R. R. (2000). Self-determination theory and the facilitation of intrinsic motivation, social development, and well-being. *The American Psychologist, 55(1),* 68.

Drake, J. (2009). *Vaccination Horror: An anthology of important works on vaccination pseudoscience.* CA: Createspace.

Eisenstein, Mayer M.D. (2008). *Don't vaccinate before you educate.* CMI Press.

Elkind, D. (2001). *The hurried child: Growing up too fast, too soon.* Cambridge, MA: DeCapo Press.

Elkind, D. (2003). *Miseducation: Preschoolers at risk.* New York: Random House.

Estroff-Marano, H. (2006, May/June). Education: Class dismissed. *Psychology Today.*

Estroff-Marano, H. (1999, July/August). The power of play. *Psychology Today.*

Gatto, J. T. (2005). *Dumbing us down: The hidden curriculum of compulsory schooling.* Canada: New Society Publishers.

Gatto, J. T. (2006). *The underground history of American education: An investigation into the prison of modern schooling.* New York: The Oxford Village Press.

Gopnik, A., Meltzoff, A. N., Kuhl, P. K. (1999). *The scientist in the crib: Minds, brains, and how children learn.* New York: William Morrow & Co.

Gupta, R., Ramji, S. (2001). Effect of delayed cord clamping on iron stores in infants born to anemic mothers: A randomized controlled trial. *Indian Pediatrics, 39,* 130-135.

Haley, Boyd (2001). *Committee for Government Reform presented on May 23, 2001 by Boyd Haley, Professor and Chair, Department of Chemistry, University of Kentucky*

Healy, J. M. (1990). *Endangered minds: Why children don't think and what we can do about it.* New York: Simon & Schuster

Henderlong, J. (2002). The effects of praise on children's intrinsic motivation. *Psychological Bulletin,* 128(5), 774-795.

Henderson, S. (2002). The correlates of inventor motivation, creativity and achievement. *Stanford University,* 142 pages, AAT 3067866.

Hennessey, B. (2003). The social psychology of creativity. *Scandinavian Journal of Educational Research, 47(3),* 253-71.

Hirsh-Pasek, K., Ph.D. Golinkoff, R. M., Ph.D. (2003). *Einstein never used flashcards: How our children really learn and why they need to play more and memorize less.* Holtzbrinck Publishers.

References

Howenstine, James, M.D. (2009). Why you should avoid taking vaccines. http://www.safe2use.com/ca-ipm/09-29-07.htm

Hutton, E., PhD, Hassan, E. S. (2007). Late vs. early clamping of the umbilical cord in full-term neonates: Systematic review and meta-analysis of controlled trials. *The Journal of the American Medical Association. 297*, 1241-1252.

Kasser, T., & Ryan, R. M. (1996). Further examining the American dream: Differential correlates of intrinsic and extrinsic goals. *Personality and Social Psychology Bulletin, 22,* 280-287

Kohn, A. (2003). Studies find reward often no motivator: Creativity and intrinsic interest diminish if task is done for gain. *Boston Globe.* Retrieved August 18, 2006, from http://www.gnu.org/philosophy/motivation.html

Lamb, S., Brown, L. M. (2006). *Packaging girlhood: Rescuing our daughters from marketers' schemes.* New York: St. Martin's Griffin.

Linn, S. (2004). *Consuming Kids: Protecting our children from the onslaught of marketing & advertising.* New York: Anchor Books.

Ludner, L. M. (1998). Home schooling works. *The scholastic achievement and demographic characteristics of home schooled students in 1998.* Home School Legal Defense Association.

Mendelsohn, R., M.D. (1987). *How to raise a healthy child in spite of your doctor.* New York: Ballantine Books.

Miller, Neil Z. (2002). *Vaccines: Are they really safe and effective?* Santa Fe, NM: New Atlantean Press.

Pink, D. H. (2005). *A whole new mind: Moving from the information age to the conceptual age.* New York: Penguin Group.

Piscane, A. (1996). Neonatal prevention of iron deficiency. *BMJ, 312,* 136-137.

Ruata, Charles, M.D. (1904). *A summary of the proofs that vaccination does not prevent smallpox but really increases it.* National Anti-Vaccination League, S616.

Sasco AJ, Paffenbarger RS Jr. (1985). Measles infection and Parkinson's disease. *Am J Epidemiol. 1985 Dec;122(6):1017-31.*

Tenpenny, Sherri, M.D. (2008). *Saying No to Vaccines.* NMA Media Press.

Tenpenny, Sherri, M.D. (2003). *Vaccines: What CDC Documents and Science Reveal.* RJ Media Magic.

Vansteenkiste, M., Ryan, R.M. and Deci, E.L. (2008) `Self-determination theory and the explanatory role of psychological needs in human well-being', in L. Bruni, F. Comim and M. Pugno (eds), Capabilities and Happiness, pp. 187-223. Oxford: Oxford University Press

Volpe, Arturo, M.D. (2009). Natural health solutions. http://www.doctorvolpe.com/

Willis, J. (2007). Preserve the child in every learner. *Kappa Delta Pi, 44(1),* 33-37.

References

Wolk, S. (2001). The benefits of exploratory time. *Educational Leadership, 59(2),* 56-9.

World Health Organization (1996). *Care in Normal Birth: A Practical Guide.*

Made in the USA
Charleston, SC
15 October 2011